T0198648

AuthorHouse™
1663 Liberty Drive
Bloomington, IN 47403
www.authorhouse.com
Phone: 1 (800) 839-8640

Published by AuthorHouse 01/13/2018

ISBN: 978-1-5462-2464-8 (sc)
ISBN: 978-1-5462-2485-3 (e)

Print information available on the last page.

This book is printed on acid-free paper.

It's the People

Spanish Fork Fiesta Days 2014

WRITTEN BY SUSAN BARBER
PHOTOS PROVIDED BY ERIC MELANDER

authorHOUSE®

SPANISH FORK WAS SETTLED BY THE "PIONEERS."
Now when most people think of pioneers, they
think of the struggles and the sacrifices of the
past. The sacrifice and struggling is a huge part,
yes, but to this day pioneers are still a large
part of our community. We can all be pioneers
by having faith and doing the right thing, and
by being leaders to those who need one.

Neisha Coutlee

This book is dedicated to all the wonderful people who have lived, now live, and will hopefully live for a long time in our part of Utah Valley. Included here are memories and stories that have been shared with each other for years.

Spanish Fork, Lake Shore and
Palmyra is home to us all!

IN ORDER TO APPRECIATE THE PRESENT, WE MUST EMBRACE THE PAST.

Every year, the city of Spanish Fork has a weeklong celebration, complete with parades, dances, craft fairs, sidewalk sales, fireworks and a rodeo. The committee of volunteers always chooses a theme for the event. In the summer of 2014, the theme was I Love this Town. Those who were new to town perhaps didn't understand the depth of feeling in this simple statement. Spanish Fork contains people who are related to some of the original settlers of this area. They have grown up together, married, built homes, done business, planted fields and gardens and taken water turns together. They do love this town. I've spoken to many of the stalwart, remaining people from all different points of town. They have told me stories of the beginnings of this town as well as the efforts taken to keep its spirit alive. Spanish Fork will not become a cardboard cutout community. These people will not allow it. In spite of the beleaguered sighs of the younger benefactors of the resilient founders, our town will grow but some things will not be forgotten. The people will not let that happen.

—*Susan Barber*

INTRODUCTION

This is a collection of memories. Some of the following memories are the exact memories of one person. Some of the stories are compiled of short memories of several people. In the process of gathering and putting these memories together I have had some enlightening and informative discussions with people as well just plain hysterical sessions where everyone had a great time but there was not much real information of consequence acquired.

An example of a nonproductive conversation with two or more people would go like this:

1st person: "Oh! I will never forget the time. . . . We were going to teach that kid in our class, what was his name? The one with the big cowlick in his hair?"

2nd person: "You mean Timmy? No, wait, you must be talking about Kate's youngest, the one with that beautiful black hair? I can't remember his name; didn't he marry Sheila and then finally ended up in Texas with Carol?"

3rd person: "Are you talking about Sheila that lived just off 300 West? Who was her Dad? I had him in school. Meanest guy ever. I think he drank spit every morning for breakfast just to make him meaner."

1st person: "No, not black hair, red. We used to call him Doody so we could say, 'Howdee Doodie!'" [laughs]

2nd person: "No, Carol went to Salt Lake with that doctor. You're talking about my cousin's wife's sister-inlaw. The only one I remember living on 3rd West was that kid whose mom made that horrible green stuff and always tried to give it away as a treat! Yuck!"

1st person: "Oh Yeah, I had that guy for Social Studies. Sometimes he did come off with some funny jokes. He even told some great stories. I didn't think he was too mean. It's just you he hated! Haha!"

3rd person: "Was he the one who used to pull the shades, turn off the lights, and sit on top of his desk on Halloween to tell us a creepy story? He was so cool! I'd jump out of my skin, but I'd had to act cool for the girls."

2nd person: "Yeah buddy, we knew you were shakin' in your boots just like the rest of us!" *[End of interview]*

1st person: " Wait, wait! Now I know who he was…"

The important thing I learned in all of this is that everyone remembers what was important to them at the time. It's like looking at snowflakes. I predict that when you read some of these stories you may remember parts of that time vividly, while the rest sits in a totally different part of your personal story. Perhaps you won't remember it at all. My suggestion; read something, then let a friend or family member read it. Then talk about it. Each may come up with something totally different. These are memories!

Here is a note to someone who is new to town. Perhaps you have wondered why the people speak or act the way they do. Perhaps you have wondered why some things may have little worth to you but other people hold them very close. Hopefully some of these stories will explain why. Some of the people in this town have heard stories themselves about when their grandpa set the stone on the first meeting house. Perhaps some of the folks like to remember the simple things in life, like hard work, hard water.

Dialect Vs Vocabulary

When several nationalities and cultures begin to intermingle, frequently there are misunderstandings or misconceptions that bring confrontation. Over time, these words, phrases and or expressions become understandable and eventually accepted. Now, when newcomers visit Spanish Fork, they will hear some unfamiliar speech patterns. Examples of some but not all include:

Usedtacould: previously, I was able or allowed to

Upandwent: a decision was acted upon

I seen: the explanation of a previous sight

Bath the kids: bathe the children

Mondee, Tewsdee, Wenzdee, Thirzdee, Sadderdee: days of the week

Gunna: going to

Shuddah: should have

Cuddah: possibly could have, or alternative action

Wooddah: if I had longer to think about it and had thought harder, possibly a more correct action would have resulted

Wood ja borrow: a request for a loan of service or money

Ta: to

Taday, tamorrow: this day and the next day

Yesturdee: the previous day

Boyack, *or* boyick: same family; no one seems to know the difference

Lade-ur: later

We was: a group action in the past tense

Ignernt: rude or ignorant

EXAMPLE: "We was gunna go fishin' taday but he upandwent yesterdee and we shore cuddah Sadderdee if you'd of borrowed me some bait cuz we shudda got there yesturdee before the Boyicks cuz I seen 'em jest past Spanish Fark furst waard. Fer ignernt!"

(If this all makes perfect sense to you, blame your grandpa!)

TABLE OF CONTENTS

Chapter 1:
How Did We Begin?

PLAY TIME. Before the electronic age, the children in Spanish Fork never lacked for playtime. Of course, they worked hard. But they could play just as hard. Some of the play was simple. Some was organized and competitive, and some was just messy and silly.

WINTER

In the winter, the children threw the usual snowballs. But sometimes they weren't just the soft fluffy snowballs tossed Hallmark-style at each other's smiling faces while chuckling softly. No, sometimes the snowballs became ice balls and were hurled viciously at one another. It was difficult to escape because by that time of year the snow had really piled up and had a crusty ice coating that could cause you to slide sideways into the gutter that hid bitter cold water just below the thin ice sheet. The boys usually built ice huts or igloos.

Then they would defend them from each other like war lords.

One year a scout master took his troop up the canyon to a lovely cabin. The scout master settled the boys inside all warm and comfy and then with no invitation went outside and built himself a snow cave. The boys were so intrigued that they joined him. They would build a fire, then stomp it out causing the inside of the cave to ice over like caulking.

The troop enlarged the cave and they could even put heaters inside. No one slept inside the lovely cabin! The best snow expedition was the year of *The Great Winter*. That year, it just kept snowing and snowing. The city crews could not keep roads clear and had no place to put all the plowed snow. So, the city contracted with Walt Limb Construction to use their heavy loaders and movers to dump all the plowed snow on an empty lot at the bottom of Wolfhollow Street. What a glorious sight! The neighborhood boys tunneled into the huge piles of snow and wound around and around, adding small caves and a few outlets. It was great fun. Did the City know the risk involved? Did the parents know what the kids were doing? Seriously?

There was a time when there was an ice skating pond down by where the County Fair Exhibition Pavilion resides now. This was a "bring your own skates and go home for hot chocolate" type of place. There was no fee for this happy place. You did not have to make reservations. Sometimes it was crowded, sometimes not so much. If it was too crowded, you could sit by the fire and wait for a spell. Some folks would get done and it would be your turn. The boys checked out the girls and vice versa. So, as was said in *The Spanish Fork Press*, "A good time was had by all!" The citizens of Spanish Fork have proposed to the City Council the return of the skating rink. However, now the rules, fees, regulations, zoning and building codes are prohibitive.

Another winter tradition was the Christmas tree bonfire up above The Wolfhollow. The Wolfhollow is a small ravine just off Scenic Drive. The farmers from the low lands by the Spanish Fork River used to drive the wolves off the pastures 5 up into the ravine, trap them and kill them. In the 1970's many families still had real live Christmas trees. They would take down the tree decorations, vacuum all the dead, dry, prickly yellow needles and throw the tree out to the street in hopes that the city would pick it up, haul it away and make it disappear.

In the Wolfhollow neighborhood, however, everyone who chose to be included would drag their dead tree down to the bottom of the street at the edge of the hill and make a huge pile. Then the families would gather at the tree pile armed with lighter fluid, matches, marshmallows and hot dogs. There was no real organization, no broadcast e-mail or organizer. It just happened (Note: this was before the Grinch movie so the neighborhood children did NOT hold hands in a circle and sing).

Nowadays, Spanish Fork has a much more benign celebration; "The Light Parade" down Main Street. Businesses and families decorate trucks or floats with lights. The Spanish Fork Police close off Main Street for ten blocks. People set up chairs and serve each other hot chocolate (or something). They yell, clap and cheer for each entry as it slowly passes by. On a good year, there are no large gaps in the parade lineup. The best entry is voted on by the public. Of course, Santa Clause is the signal that the parade is over and the Christmas/holiday season has officially begun!

Spanish Fork City itself also has a huge holiday event at the Canyon View Park at the mouth of Spanish Fork Canyon. This is called "The Festival of Lights." The entire park is beautifully decorated with holiday lights and some action figures that are timed to the special music you can tune to in your car. It is possible To arrange for flat-bed trailers to load with entire families (you must provide your own family.) People come from literally miles away to see this event. It is held for the entire holiday season until New Year's Day and gets bigger and better every year!

SPRING
When Spring came, the scent in the air changed. There were still crunchy snow patches on the shady side of the corral in Lakeshore as Jed tossed the saddle onto the horse's back and secured the soft, spicy-scented strap around Beck's underside. The half-frozen mud

was treacherous to walk in. One foot could slide over a slippery dirt clod while the other foot would sink down into cold, melted, watery dung. This was going to be a long day for the manger—in fact the whole yard would look really different in about twelve hours.

This morning, the yard and pasture in Lakeshore was full of cattle. They were kind of anxious as if they could tell something was going to happen. The mother cows were bawling for their calves, trying to locate their young waiting…for something. When Jed was all ready and had the provisions in his saddle bags that he would need, he called a "Good bye" to his wife, tightened the cinch and saddled up.

Jed's family owned ground up Spanish Fork Canyon around Diamond Fork, and some of his neighbors in Lakeshore also either owned ground or had grazing permits allowing them to send their cattle to spend the hot summers up in the cool canyon. They were all herded up Highway 6, going towards Denver. Some of the herd would be cut out as they arrived at certain ranches. The animals would spend the summer in the cooler hills, foraging on the grasses and drinking from the streams, and later, in the fall, when the water master notified the ranchers, the cattle would be rounded up and driven back down the narrow, two-lane highway to the drive corrals on Canyon Road. Then the ranchers would have to go to the drive corrals, retrieve their stock and drive them home.

This sounds easy, but it was really a huge project. Picture this: hundreds of slow-moving animals sauntering down 300 South to Main Street, turning right, then slowly moving to 400 North and on down to Lakeshore, with some herds dropping off in Palmyra on the way. Traffic would be at a standstill and the streets lined with carloads of youngsters and moms cheering on their "men folks." However, it was always a fun day for the local kids who could sit by the side of the road and try to guess which brand belonged to which rancher and just what the brand meant. That was so cool, what would it be? Intertwined letters, diamond S or stacked rafters?

Jed patted his saddlebags just to remind himself that he had stashed a Big Hunk candy bar in there that he would gnaw on all the way up the canyon. Thankfully he didn't bring a chocolate bar like he did the first year. What a mess! He gently whistled for his dog and moved the herd out onto 400 North where he was joined by his neighbors. They moved along, joking with each other and speculating on the time it would take to complete this project.

The drive went off without a hitch as they dropped off the last herd and turned around to begin their return trip down the canyon. Jed had devoured his lunch and cleaned out his treats. The cowboys had to eat lunch without stopping because the cattle were slowing down the highway traffic and if they stopped to eat they ran the chance of some crazy steer wandering off the edge of the road and likely falling into the river. The men joked about who would have to go into the river to rescue the steer. Pity the new guy, whoever he was! Sometimes, after much debate, it was determined that if there was some sort of crisis, the guy with the worst batting average last season would need to be the "rescuer."

As Jed and his weary horse padded into the empty yard the dogs gave a rousing "welcome home" chorus. The yard was different as Jed has expected. The snow patches had melted, leaving even more slushy mud around the manger. The corral and surrounding pasture had a green sheen with the promise of new growth. Jed knew it had only been a day since he'd left, but in his eye, the pasture did have a hint of promise of a good season and a good crop. Farmers and ranchers are constant optimists.

Spring was also the beginning of Baseball season. Spanish Fork is a huge baseball presence in the state. Before there were three high schools in the Nebo District, Spanish Fork High School had captured seven regional championships between 1985 and 1999, and one state championship in 1988. The youth begin learning and playing baseball when they start Kindergarten and will play on a team in the City Recreation Department until they make the high school ball team. Grown men in the barbershop in town can quote stats from their own years on the field!

Everyone has their own memories of that certain game or great play. Sometimes the memories are different even when it was the same game. Special memories are often repeated, especially ones from the Sunshine Tournament played in St. George every year like. "that day, the Binks kid—I think it was Aaron—who hit the ball out of the park, into and then out of the school bus!" Few remember the exact details.

Spanish Fork loves the coaches; some men in town have coached for years and years. Once a team of little ten-yearolds reenacted a scene from the Disney movie *Angels in the Outfield*. When the team only had six players, including a tenyear- old pitcher, they faced an opponent with a full team. But the pitcher, Derek Larsen, held them and the little team won the game! Derek kept playing in the city teams until he made the high school team where he played until he graduated and then moved on to play college ball. Travelers used to be able to see Derek's picture on a billboard on Highway 6 going up Spanish Fork Canyon.

This community has had families who have all played for the high school at some time. With the growth in town and now three high schools there still exists baseball families. Those little boys grow up and have children of their own who also play baseball. Oh! How we love our ball players!

For some, the games stop when high school does. For others, the games go on and the players and their games just get bigger. One example is Steve Gardner. He was coached in little league by Jack Swenson, and continued to be coached by dedicated volunteer coaches and dads in this town until he made the high school team where he was coached until he graduated in 1966. After graduation, he played ball on the Weber State team for three years and was "All Conference" and was then drafted to play professionally for the Houston Astros for three seasons where he won the Western Carolina League Batting Championship and was named "Louisville Slugger" in 1971.

Steve left the professional baseball team to become a teacher and coach himself at Bonneville High School in Ogden, Utah for seven years. He left Bonneville High School to become the head baseball coach at Snow College for eight years. He must have still had strong ties pulling him back to his hometown, because he returned to Utah County to be the head baseball coach and teacher at Utah Valley University (UVU). To his credit, he has achieved 647 collegiate wins in his coaching career. Steve Gardner received the Wilson W. Sorensen Lifetime Achievement Award at UVU and was nominated to the Utah Sports Hall of Fame.

Just think—this all started in Little League in Spanish Fork! And while all this baseball was going on, don't forget the boys in "the back parking lot!" These were the boys in the shop, the ones with the big, noisy trucks. The ones who fixed tractors and then raced them, and then raised money so they could build something even bigger and louder!

The back parking lot was also home for the Future Farmers of America (FFA). Here, they learned how to raise livestock and how to drive the eighteen-wheel semi-trucks to haul them to market. They had a great time learning how to raise crops which might someday feed the entire community. They also learned how to compete in the Rodeos.

"Rodeo" in Spanish Fork has its own set of rules. For example, in December when the Mayor, City Council, City Department heads and Fiesta Days Rodeo Director go down to Las Vegas to the National Rodeo Association, they all dress exactly the same; white dress shirt, black pants, and black vest. Cowboys dressed like that are very polite and businesslike while they negotiate with stock handlers and facilitators. They probably learned this deportment in FFA.

THE SPANISH FORK - SALEM AREA CHAMBER OF
COMMERCE
EXECUTIVE DIRECTOR MESSAGE
by Clark H. Caras

Spanish Fork and Salem have always been the home
to winners and in the past month we've seen that
tradition repeated several times in sports, including
rodeo along with baseball and softball, in business with
ribbon cuttings and storefront openings, and in civic
pride with a golf tournament providing more than 20
high school seniors with scholarships, and the official

kickoff of the Chamber sponsored 2015 Play Unplugged program, along with the voting by thousands from our communities and around the nation that sees state Farm Insurance awarding $25,000 ensuring Chamber involvement with the movement for years to come!

And for myself the importance of all this is not so much "the winning" but the involvement and pride of the entire communities and population. For with that has come proof of the unity of "community" which for me is what the Chamber is all about. Unity of pride and the progress that comes with pulling together, whether for the cheering on of the three boys baseball teams and a girls softball champion; or the excitement of getting neighbor and friends involved in voting on Facebook every day in the hope of bringing the guarantee of a proven youth program to 101 business doors for more years to come and Bragg Tags galore.

With the smell of first crop hay in the air even on Main Street and on the shores of Salem Pond, my message this month is congratulations to the Spanish Fork High School baseball team and its State Championships, congratulations to Salem Hills and Maple Mountain High Schools who literally and figuratively were right there with them; congratulations to the Spanish Fork High School Girls Softball team and its State Championship, congratulations to the 20+ high school seniors from all four high schools in our Chamber reach who have been awarded a $1500 scholarship from our Chamber and the Spanish Fork Rotary Club made possible by the efforts of more than 30 golf teams who braved thunder and lightning at Spanish Oaks and represented some of our finest businesses and businessmen and women in the area.

Congratulations and a shout out goes to the Diamond Fork Riding Club and Spanish Fork's Park and Recreation Department for seeing the second year of a sellout at the new Spanish Fork Rodeo Arena as the community welcomed the nation's top cowboys and cowgirls in the Justin Boot sponsored Champion's Challenge.

And thanks to CBS Sports the entire nation was introduced to the beauty and excitement of what surrounds these neighborhoods and businesses as well as the unity of community as it cheered on many Of its homegrown talent in the world championship rodeo, yes, in the last 30 days we've seen ribbons cut in front of three Spanish Fork Main Street store fronts; that in their own way are champions for taking the chance and opening new doors in the promise of the building of unity among clients and customers served. And last, but definitely not least; most definitely not, we have seen the efforts of Colt Sampson and his team at State Farm; unite a community and its people in an effort to take advantage of the great program a stand out national company such as State Farm does in sharing dollars made, $25,000 to be exact, but only if they are earned. And earned indeed they were; by 10 votes a day on Facebook by folks from north Main to the top of Elkridge and beyond.

SUMMER

Grandma's house smelled wonderful that morning! There were flowers of different colors and fragrances everywhere, with the different shades of green leaves and stems scattered all around the screen porch and out to the patio. I walked through the kitchen trying only to step on the flat long leaves that looked like Indian feathers. Grandma was sitting on a milking stool, clipping quickly and separating the flowers by size and humming under her breath. She looked up, smiling and said, "You look like you are dancing across the room!"

She handed me a small set of scissors and a large stack of wonderful smelling flowers of all shades of pink. "Cut them off about right here, and place them in that water bucket over there. Oh, and while you're at it, take my stack of cut flowers over to the bucket too, please." She explained that we needed to hustle because Grandpa was due back in with another huge bundle of cut flowers. We were going to arrange these flowers in 70 containers of different sizes and then take them to the cemetery this morning because it was Memorial Day and Heaven forbid, someone got missed!

This is the way summer began. School was out until Labor Day. I wondered, who decided to start and end the Summer with a special holiday each, the moms or the teachers?

Taking the flowers to the cemetery with Grandma was fun. She was a no-nonsense deliverer. We would take the flowers, be sure they had plenty of water and on to the next one, with a stop at the water faucet to refill the water jug. Not so, with my mother. In the years past, if I didn't time it just right, I would have to go in my mom's car. She would take the flowers to the grave site, fuss with them just a little and then visit with anyone and everyone in the general vicinity! It took forever.

Once the cemetery was properly decorated, we went home for a rest and so Mom could finish preparing the food for the cookout at my other grandmother's. I always looked forward to this because my uncle would let us cousins get into the hammock that was tied to the big tree and he would push us so hard that the hammock would go around and around until we were tied up tight inside. We thought it was hilarious, but now I'm thinking there was a method to his madness. The barbecue always came replete with cheeseburgers, potato salad and best of all, watermelon!

The summertime between holidays was filled with adventures. Some mornings, if we had slept over at one of the grandparent's, we could help gather the eggs. I was afraid of some of the chickens, but it was so amazingly lucky if I happened to reach under the hen and she would just rise up and lay that egg right into my hand! My grandpa always told me the same joke every time I went with him to gather the eggs; "That's not gum on the floor... don't eat it," he'd say. And then he'd laugh, once really loud, and then quietly chuckle.

After breakfast, my grandmother would get me started on washing the dishes. While I was drying the dishes, Grandma would go to the kitchen door and toss the soapy water right out onto the dusty driveway. Look out dogs and cats! Good thing she didn't live in town. Then we could play the rest of the day. We could do just about anything we wanted and we usually did. Some days, we floated in the canal on an inner tube, some days we fished in the creek (or crick) and if it was rainy we could talk our parents into taking us swimming at Park-Ro She or Arrowhead. That was always a tossup. We liked both places for an indoor pool. It mostly depended on which way our parents wanted to go; Benjamin or Springville.

On good, hot days, it was fun to go to the Spanish Fork Pool. And, of course, all summer, there were millions of baseball games going on. We were playing, watching, or putting together our own team to play a game. At nightfall, we liked to play night games like Kick the Can, Hide and Seek, toilet papering, "xxxxx-knocking," or "knock and run" (the alliteration was more fun, though politically incorrect) I didn't even know it was a problem. The older kids played kissing tag, which is a stupid game, in my opinion, because everyone knew who could be caught as well as who nobody wanted to catch.

Every summer day was a build up to July 24th, because after the celebration was over it seemed as though the summer was over. The ball games were finished and the stores started to hold back-to-school sales. Visiting relatives packed up and went home. The weather was so hot, I wondered if that is why they called it "The Dog Days of Summer." Even the dogs didn't want to play; it was too hot.

EXECUTIVE DIRECTOR'S MESSAGE FOR JULY
NEWSLETTER OF THE SPANISH FORK SALE AREA
CHAMBER OR COMMERCE.
by Clark H. Caras

Growing up in Spanish Fork the words "Fiesta Days" were magic to me because it was like Christmas in July! And with Grandpa and Grandma Harrison living a half block off Main Street on 5th North it was like being right in the middle of it all.

Overnight American flags began fluttering up and down the boulevard and even as a kid you knew that red, white and blue signaled something important and special. And especially when that brand new Memorial

Building was home to men who could talk about Iwo Jima, D-Day and a reverent place called Pearl Harbor. And to be blessed with that famous Canyon Wind that every morning brought those pieces of cloth to attention and made them snap to remind you they were there!

And then on that very special day, as exciting as standing in front of Forsey's the day after Thanksgiving and waving to Santa; the carnival would snake its way south down Main to jaw-dropping slobbers of excitement as it would roll past the Frost Top, World Drug, and Gift Fair, to the sacred ground of Center Street's west side.

Then as the Ferris Wheel rose from its trailer to become the highest point in town, it was like an unheard whistle had blown and merchants up and down the way began rolling everything you'd ever wanted out front doors of stores onto sidewalks that suddenly had no cracks. And families were drawn to the center of town to wander the maze of color and new smell in this transformation of turning a store inside out and the sidewalk sale became as celebratory as the Mammoth Parade.

Spanish Fork suddenly was the magnet drawing friends and family from Benjamin, Lake Shore, Palmyra, Leland, as yes, even family and friends from Salem were allowed to bring their dollar and meet you at the new library and venture into the mechanical smells and deco colored carnival with aroma of corn dogs, cotton candy, and sticky red candy apples.

Fiesta Days meant new boots, and a new yoked cowboy shirt with new snap buttons. And a one night trip into the grandstand of the rodeo grounds; that wooden underbelly and tall fences became the best playground in the world for a bunch of kids celebrating pioneer ancestors crossing the plains, and yes—the slivers were worth it!

Fish ponds made of sheets, dunk tanks at the park, and a parade just for kids down Center Street all downhill required nothing to enter but a squeaky bike and a bit of crepe paper in the spokes.

A jump in the new pool at the high school, a pronto pup or brown topper and barbecue at Grandpa's and Fiesta Days (aka Christmas in July) was done.

FALL

Autumn is the saddest season of the year, in my esteemed, ten-year-old opinion. Parents and teachers alike declare that summer vacation is over as soon as the last blast of the Fiesta Days fireworks display reverberates over the West Mountain. The leaves on the trees dry up, die and float to the ground even after a desperate attempt to attract positive attention by changing into a vast array of beautiful colors. They are raked, blown, bagged, and hauled to the compost pile without even an apology or a showing of gratitude for the months of singing breezes and shady respite from the glowering sun.

The merchants try to capitalize on the season, first by offering "back-to-school bargains," followed closely with Halloween costumes, masks, and scary decorations. The merchants must feel a bit guilty for trying to capitalize on our childish pain at loosing the fun-filled summer days because they follow the black witches, bats and ghosts with lovely warm Thanksgiving sweetness portrayed in rich, warm colors and a picture of a steaming pumpkin pie.

We children are not fooled! We accept your offer of free little candy bars and candy corn given in exchange for our freedom to run, swim, play outside and enjoy the still warm, beautiful days. We return to our parents' schedules of dance, gymnastics, and music lessons. We willingly abandon awakening after the sun has risen, and retiring just as it is again beginning to rise.

We, the children, do all this because… it is football season! We love our football teams, especially now that we have so many different teams surrounding us. Once there was a football team for each town. So it was easy. If you lived in Spanish Fork, you went to and cheered for Spanish Fork High School. Likewise, if you lived in Salem, you attended and cheered for Spanish Fork High School. The same situation existed for the Springville and Mapleton people. Now, in the current year (2015), there are four high schools between Salem and Springville. The college schools are also stretching our allegiance. Once, a family only had to choose to be loyal to Brigham Young University (BYU) or University of Utah. Sometimes the selection was one of logistics. You cheered for the school closest to your home. Now, with the assistance of the Electronic Age, a house can be divided according to whose device will pick up which game.

Besides football, the fall season offers us, the children, hunting season, fall break, UEA Convention, LDS conference weekend and pre-Christmas wish lists! If you add in homecoming football games in four different high schools and four homecoming dances, some of the parents are beginning to succumb to the hectic pace and seek any sort of uncomplicated quiet. This is great for the ten-year-old set! Now, we can plan sleepovers, days at Grandma's, and weekends with no projects because the poor parents are exhausted. Our game plan is to quietly whisper Christmas wishes just to see Mom and Dad cringe a little.

No matter the season, the weather, or the time of day, a tenyear-old can seek out and find plenty of free entertainment.

Chapter 2:
Then and Now

The Winona—The Old Opera House
by B. Davis Evans; April 4, 1968

Dear Reader:

My humble message for today has been churning around in the channels of my mind for many weeks, so now is the time to bring it out into the open and organize it into some kind of a message and I hope it stirs up the nostalgic memories of my generation, the generation before mine and the generation before that….

It's the story of Spanish Fork's old opera house, "The Winona." It was located between First and Second North on Main. The front entrance was about where the vacant DTR building now stands. A long corridor, about 12 feet wide, went back a hundred feet (give or take a foot) to the ticket booth thence through a couple of doors to the slanted floored auditorium, with its grand old balcony at the rear. The place seated 850 patrons (give or take a couple).

At the west end was the high-ceilinged stage with a sunken orchestra pit in front of it. The stage was crude in comparison with what we have now, but to me it was a "bit of heaven," as the Irish would say. It had four rows of lights—green, red, blue, and white; each color was connected to a dimming circuit. It also had a row of footlights along the front of the stage. Footlights, sort of a symbol for the stage, have long since given way to the high powered lights that are shot from the auditorium now.

The first show I remember seeing on that stage was a musical extravaganza of local talent. I sat on my mother's knee and was fascinated beyond words, my brother Joe was a member of the song and dance group that did a swing number. Four girls in dresses of the Gay Nineties, sat on swings and four fellows in dark coats, white trousers and straw hats got to swinging those gals and they flew right past the curtain line smack dab over the orchestra pit. I'd never seen anything like it. Gradually the swings slowed down and the gals got out and then right before our eyes the swings went up into the ceiling. Each fellow then took a girl and they danced around the stage to real live music. You know, from that time on I compared screen and stage stars to "me big brudder Joe." Yes, Rudolph Valentino, Wallace Reid, Conrad Nagel and others were handsome, but they couldn't sing, act, or dance any better that "me big brudder Joe."

That was my first experience in the old Winona but not the last. I don't think I ever missed a stage performance of any kind for many years.

I suppose, more than any other group, the high school musicals and plays made use of the hall in its last days.

… An Interesting aspect of the hall was the old ugly asbestos fire curtain that separated the stage from the audience. When 31 one arrived early for a performance, one sat and studied the picture on that curtain. As I recall it was painted in different shades of brown. It was a painting of an old boat beached on the trashy banks of a river; an old stone bridge loomed in the background. It was almost enough to ruin a good show (I'll bet if Arvil Huff had been around then, that picture wouldn't have stayed there long).

But in spite of its ugliness, I loved it. I guess I did so because it was part of the old opera house.

Another interesting feature of the place was the grape clusters, yes—I said grape clusters—that made a border up next to the ceiling. They were plaster casts about 14 inches from leaf to tip and eight inches wide at the top. Gee, I'd like to have gotten one of those clusters when the place went down. I'd have framed it and hung it in my home.

The only thing I disliked about those grapes was that they extended up around the balcony and occasionally some of the boys who sat up there would dig a grape off with his knife and toss it at the performers. It didn't do much good to complain to Jabe Faux. He would say, "Get out there and perform so well that they'll forget about the grapes." You know, he was right. If a guy survived the first ten minutes after the curtain went up, he'd generally make it.

Well the old house fell. It gradually deteriorated. The last time I was in there, it was a storehouse for onions. I didn't stay long; one look was enough. What an ignoble end for a grand old hose. I suppose old buildings have to go to make way for the new, but some of the past could be spared. The old Angels has been spared and what good is it? Why couldn't it have been the Winona? After all, part of it was one of the city's first church buildings.

April 25, 1968

Dear Reader:

A few weeks ago I stirred up some dead or dying memories pertaining to the Winona Theater. Since that time, I have had many people volunteer further information on the subject. I would like to share some of that information with you.

The Spanish Fork Opera House, as it was originally called was opened on February 16, 1911, by the Moore-Ethier Company. Ezra Warner informed me that the dramatic company was named for a man-and-wife team; whether Moore and Ethier were first or last names; no one seems to be sure. This company presented "The Red Cross Nurse" February 16, 17, 18.

Now the building from which the opera house sprung was originally called
the Central Meeting House. Its corner stones were laid
May 18, 1863, and the building was dedicated in 1875.
This was a united effort of the citizens
of the city. The Central Meeting House held church as well
as city meetings.

The City Pavilion—Palmour Ball Room
by B. Davis Evans; November 23, 1967

Dear Reader:

Once upon a time a building stood on the east end of our city park. For many years it was known as "The City Pavilion." It was the gathering place for many city functions. It was constructed long before the turn of the century.

It was my lucky lot to be a teenager in the thirties when that building became one of Utah County's more popular dance halls. It was renamed "The Palmour Ball Room," "The Escalante Gardens" and maybe more names that I no longer remember, but for many years it was the headquarters of the valley's dancing crowds; every Saturday night, from September to May that building rocked with the pounding of hundreds of dancing feet on that beautiful hardwood floor.

I'm not sure of the size of the building but it must have covered an acre or two. I had the privilege of putting a false ceiling there a couple of times. It seemed more like a five acre plot then. Three or four potbellied stoves were found sporadically around the hall. They could heat up the air well within 14 or 15 feet but in other parts of the hall one could see his steaming breath on a cold night. I suppose that was the reason we had so many dancing young people at that time; they couldn't stand around like they do now or they would freeze to death.

Well, now that I've laid the footings of my message, I want to say something.

At this time of year a wave of nostalgia comes upon me that almost freezes up the breath of life. When I drive past the park, I often mentalize that old structure and sometimes I think I hear the strains of My Blue

Heaven as it was once played by Verdi Brienholt and his 16-piece orchestra.

Only we who frequented that hall during the thirties can appreciate that old building and what transpired there.

We had the privilege of dancing 16 times per evening and on New Year's Eve 32 times. A guy had to be in pretty good condition to survive 32 dances each with a different girl (We didn't dance all evening with the same girl just because we took her to the "shindig").

A word about New Year's Dances; One orchestra couldn't play from 9 p.m. to 4 a.m., so at 12:31 a second orchestra took the stand and played till four o'clock in the morning.

Now may I comment on the music. Beautiful numbers were played then that we would hum all week long, or maybe even sing quietly, along with the orchestra into the ear of the cute little chick (I'd like to hear one number that the youth dance to today that is worth remembering even for a few days).

Friends of the thirties, do you remember *Are You Lonesome Tonight?, In a Little Spanish Town, Waiting for Ships That Never Come In, Piccolo Pete* and a thousand others that when they were played even I, who had two left feet, could dance.

Well, the grass and shrubs are growing now where the old hall stood, but regardless of what is placed on the park's east side, I shall never forget that old dance hall that meant so much to me and a few thousand others like me.

Portions of it still stand out on Gill Bearnson's cattle ranch on the old Payson Road. Whenever I pass that way, I slow down a bit to pay my respects to what is left of a grand old hall.

So, I'll say, "Goodnight sweetheart 'til we meet tomorrow. Goodnight sweetheart, sleep will banish sorrow; tears in parting will make us forlorn, but with the dawn a new day is born…" No one could forget that one. It was the last number played at each dance. When we heard that one, we knew that it was time to go home.

Wow! Since then, dancing has changed many times. To name a few, the "Boogie" Moonwalk, and Limbo. Now people just move shoulders, then legs and feet, all while smiling at their partner and holding a drink or chips in one hand and even sometimes turning completely around to stealthily catch a glance from across the room at another prospect. It isn't necessary and is 35 sometimes impossible for dance partners to communicate. The room is filled with noise, the beat and the words are so fast. If you were to slow down the words you would hear that it is poetry, it rhymes, but what does it mean? The meaning depends on the beat. Is this an improvement?

The City Pavilion did come down. It was replaced with swing sets and a half-moon shaped shrubbery set up on the southeast corner. The shrubbery arrangement became a convenient place for young lovers to meet in private (at least it was private for a short time). Then picnic tables and playground equipment were placed on that side of the park. The city added a stage to the east side of the library for programs.

Right now, when there is an empty building in town people begin to speculate on the best use for said building. One repeated suggestion is a "place to dance" or " a, like, club" Oh! B. Davis Evans is smiling down on us now.

It's Deer Hunting Time!
by B. Davis Evans; October 12, 1967

Dear Reader:

It won't be long now and all the men, half the boys and onefifth of the women will deck themselves out in red, take their trusty gun in hand and head for the hills. Many will sleep on the hard ground, eat fried potatoes three times a day, scour the hills and scare up only jack rabbits, walk up steep mountain sides, beat their way through areas that would make the Sleeping Beauty Castle grounds look like a public park, get shot at, get a few wood ticks in their hide, miss Sunday school, shoot a deer (maybe), drag him for 14 miles, develop a rupture, go home and find that no one in the family likes deer meat. It's given to a neighbor and by morning their dog is chewing on your hard-earned meat.

Thousands of hunters each year cry out, "Never again! I've had enough."

But as the autumn leaves begin to turn their myriad of colors, and red shirts show up in the store windows, each of us has a stirring deep within us that whispers: "This is the year. You'll shoot one 60 yards from the road on the first morning and you'll be home in time to watch Rawhide on TV"

So, on we go year after year.

I've got venison in my deep freeze that I shot on Boulder Mountain ten years ago. We can't stand to eat it, and we hate to throw it away because I had so much trouble getting it. I carried him for five miles because Doc Peterson found a cow's skull that had a perfect set of teeth and he wanted the skull to ride in the saddle, therefore we carried the deer on our backs.

Well, such is life in our town, but we wouldn't have it any other way.

DEER HUNT?
by Douglas Houghton

What a beautiful day. Late October on the day before the deer hunt, sitting around the campfire with family and friends awaiting the big event. Stories were told and retold... some that really happened and others that none of us could remember or even believe.

I was among the storytellers and how much my good friend Doug believed I could not say. I had invited Doug on his first deer hunt, and I wanted to impress him with a great outing. Little did I know how impressed he would be before this little outing was completed.

We ate, told more stories, or rather, little white lies until well after dark when the flames of our fires were tickling the stars above. Dad finally said we better hit the sack, 4:30 a.m. would come soon enough.

Sometime during the night I was awakened by a terrific wind outside the trailer. I thought, oh great, just what we need, but I felt the wind would knock the remaining leaves from the trees and make it easier to see the deer. I fell back to sleep and was awakened by the alarm. I jumped out of bed, turned on the lights and started the stove. I quickly dressed while making sure everyone else was awake and opened the door to go visit Mother Nature. Imagine my consternation when I threw open the door and was greeted by huge, quarter-size snowflakes, and 14" of snow on the ground. Discouraged, yes, defeated no. Doug said, "Lets go back to bed!" Absolutely not, this day only comes once a year.

After dressing as warmly as we could and having a quick breakfast of hot chocolate and donuts, we trudged out into the snowstorm. Now you must remember, this was in the late 60's or early 70's. We didn't have water-proof shoes or outerwear in those days. So in a very short time we were rather soaked. Doug didn't say much about our "fun" conditions but I could feel disgust emanating from him and how he shouldn't imagine my idea of enjoyment.

We hiked and trudged through the deep snow with it falling down our necks from limbs above us. Finally after daylight arrived and with snow still falling, we tried to find a large pine tree under which we could find some shelter and build a fire. Have you ever tried to build a fire with wet matches, wet sticks, 16" of snow and with numb fingers? It doesn't work. Thus, Doug and I started our journey back to camp.

Just before we reached camp, we had to cross the creek. We didn't look for rocks or logs to cross over because we were already soaked. We just walked right through it.

While we were trying to dry out in the trailer, I found it difficult to get Doug to say much. I don't know if he was thoroughly disgusted with me or just too cold to speak. "Well," I said "It's only 364 days until next year's opener."

By the way, Doug is still my best friend.

OUR COMMUNITY'S DIVERSE ORIGINS
by B. Davis Evans; October 19, 1967

Dear Reader:

I am a "Native Son." I think that means I was born, reared, and have lived here practically all my life. Two other hidden meanings may also be present: 1. One never has gotten far enough ahead financially to leave town; 2. One may have loved the old town so much one hasn't wanted to live elsewhere. I suppose my reason for remaining here when all my old friends (other native sons) went out into the world to seek their fortunes has a smidgen of reasons 1 and 2.

The fact remains, I'm still here and the way things are shaping up, shall not leave. I now have a cemetery lot so when the hum-drum of this petty pace is done, I shall join the citizens of that beautiful silent city to the south and there I shall lie 40 until forces greater than any here has decided my next move. Hey, wait a minute. I was carried away for a minute. That's not what I wanted to write about at all. Let's get back to this "Native Son."

When I was a kid, my father grew sugar cane on our farm. We ground it up and made molasses, and then on Saturdays, during the winter, my brothers and I loaded our buggy with buckets of it and sold it from door to door. The town had a population of about 300 people which was divided into areas. The wind belt or the southeast section was Iceland. The country to the northeast was Denmark, the land to the northwest was Wales and that from the southwest was the integrated area. It was sometimes called the "Silk Stocking Area".

When I'd return from my Saturday's selling, Mother would ask where I'd sold. I wouldn't give street numbers;

I'd say I sold in Wales today and she'd say, "Yes, I can tell. You have developed the dialect."

I'm not sure why they called the southwest Section the Silk Stocking Area unless the people had more money there. I know I did sell more molasses there.

Why my mother and Father settled in Iceland, I'll never know. They were both of Welsh decent and they must have loved their nationality because they gave me two last names, Davis Evans. Anyway, I was a Welshman, reared among the Icelanders. Many people in all areas could not speak English and when the elderly Icelandic women would say "Farth la haim" I thought she was telling me that she didn't want any molasses. I found after a couple of years that she was telling me to go home.

I'll not mention some terms I learned in Wales, but I learned to grunt and slam a door in Denmark.

Now after many years, we have a San Francisco Nob Hill in Iceland, a Little Chicago in Denmark a new subdivision in Wales and an integrated high school in the integrated area.

There has always been something interesting and alive about our town and I suppose there will always be.

P.S.—We were loaded with many nationalities, but few Spaniards, yet we gave our town a Spanish name.

Note to readers; this was written in 1967. As of the year 2015 this article is fraught with political incorrectness however true and humorous.

If you are really curious about the diversity in this community you should look at the section of this book where all the old home pictures and names are listed. Map it out and you will see how true this is. Consider this fact; people packed up whatever they could and left everything else in the homeland when they immigrated to America. Then they packed it all up again and traveled hundreds of miles to settle in Spanish Fork. Doesn't it seem natural that they would want to begin this new life in the comfort of the similarity in customs and language?

RESPECTING OUR VETERANS
by B. Davis Evans; November 7, 1968

Dear Reader:

By the time this issue is in your homes, Veterans Day will not be far away. To me Veterans Day is one of the most sacred of our national holidays. It is then that we have an opportunity to pause in this hectic rush of time to pay our devotion to those men who fought and many made the supreme sacrifice that we might live in peace in a free land.

I am not in a good mood today, so if you want to read something light or humorous you must find it elsewhere. My attention was drawn recently to the cemetery marker of a friend of mine who died in battle just one month before his twenty-fifth birthday. I copied the following message from the valuable marker that stands in the Spanish Fork Cemetery in memory of him:

Maj. Waldon Williams
Army Air Corps
May 10, 1918 - April 7, 1943
Lost his life in the Pacific Area…
"Although his body is over there,
sweet memories linger here."

Set in stone beside this message is a beautiful photograph of Waldon. The picture is about six inches long and about three inches wide. I've always felt that having Waldo's picture on the marker was in very good taste, as his family didn't have his body to bury, what's wrong with having his picture in his stone? But it seems next to impossible to keep that picture in good condition. Vandals have defaced it on three occasions. Each time it is repaired, a craftsman has to remove the picture. It is sent to San Francisco for technical work, then the craftsman has to re-cement it back onto the stone. This procedure took place only a few months ago, but today

Weldon's picture is again marred, by BB or pellet shots, to the extent that another replacement job is necessary.

I was wondering if the individual or individuals who pulled that job read the message on that marker. If he had and if he bore any conscience at all, he would have thought again, "There's not a body buried here. This man disappeared in a flaming plane in the Pacific. He died that I, an American Citizen might walk these streets a free man, that I might roam the fields with my gun in hand, but did he die that I should walk into a city cemetery and deface a monument in his memory?"

Waldon Williams was a member of a respected Spanish Fork family. He was a brother of Bishop Arch Williams of Payson, Raleigh Williams, Maggie Crump and Vera Shelton of Spanish Fork and brothers who have made their communities better places because of their living in them and he too would have contributed his share to a better America had he been privileged to live.

NOW HEAR THIS: The person who would do such a dastardly deed will never accomplish as much in this life if he lives to be 70 times 70 as Waldon accomplished in his 25 years of living.

I hope this round-the-town message gets brought to the attention of them who commit such acts of vandalism and will have an influence on them for better "American activities."

I am not only pleading for the safety of Waldon's marker, but all markers that have been defaced or broken just for "the hell of it." My heart bleeds a little when I see the broken narrow type stones that, as a rule, mark the graves of our pioneers who sacrificed much to make our area livable.

Our cemeteries are sacred places and to us who have love ones buried on our little plots of ground therein revere those plots as holy ones, so please do not trespass.

The Williams family will soon have the damage on Waldon's stone repaired one more time. Please respect their wishes by looking but not touching.

There is not much we can so do for veterans. The sacrifices that most of them have made and are making are soon forgotten. The least we can do is to honor their burial places.

Well said, Mr. Evans. Except, now, in 2015, Spanish Fork is doing much more for our veterans. Stop by the cemetery on the evening proceeding Memorial Day and see at least 1500 American flags under tall bright spotlights honoring each fallen soldier buried within the cemetery. Years ago the members of the Spanish Fork American Legion began placing small white crosses in the open grassy field at the front of the cemetery, just as you entered the gates. As that project began to overwhelm the Legion members, City Councilman Richard Davis enlisted help from the young men in his ward to help place the many crosses. Pretty soon, neighbors and interested members of the community volunteered their help placing all the crosses.

Some scouts have made it their personal Eagle Scout project to repaint and repair the many crosses of the veterans! One night when the American Legion pulled the truck up, loaded with all the crosses, so many helpers converged on the project that they couldn't unload the symbols of courage fast enough. One group of volunteers built racks to perfectly fit the truck and trailer to hold all those crosses. Boy Scouts have repaired the podium for the speakers for the special ceremony held the next day at the entrance of the cemetery. I suggest you attend the ceremony on Memorial Day morning and listen to the speakers. Or for a different kind of patriotic experience, attend the flag retirement ceremony held in the Spanish Fork arena in July.

The flag retirement ceremony is amazing now. This is a real flag retirement ceremony—not a 1960's flag burning. The first time the Fiesta Days Committee tried to have a retirement ceremony, it was held by the flag pole down at the rodeo grounds. About 30 chairs were set up in a circle around where the fire was going to be. The townspeople really didn't know what to do or how to do it. So, they stood around, leaned against the walls of the old Dairy Barn shed and waited for Thad Johnson to tell them what to do.

A couple of cub scout troops were running around, looking for the marshmallows. If there is a fire and dads are standing around talking, then there should be sticks and marshmallows, right?"

Every year, the retirement ceremony has grown bigger and better. Now, the event is held under the direction of Mark Harrison and Steve Money inside the new rodeo arena. The crowd totals approximately 4500 people.

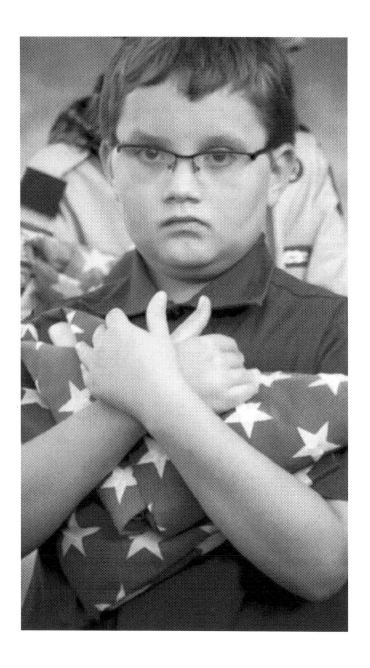

Of those people there are about 650 scouts assisted by their leaders. The C Battery of The Spanish Fork Guard consists of approximately 100 members who set up and assist with the burn site. During the course of the retirement, approximately one thousand out-of-service flags will be ceremoniously placed on the fire pit that is 25 feet wide and 40 feet long.

As the fire is brightly burning a military band plays the musical theme of each military branch. As their anthem is played, veterans of that branch of service stand to rousing applause from the crowd. The scouts begin to stomp their feet on the floor bleachers and keep pounding until it becomes a thunderous roar! The program always has a distinguished speaker who usually gets the crowd patriotically inspired. This year, in 2015, we were fortunate to hear from one of our own, Kyle Harrison, Spanish Fork High School class of 1994, who is a Master Sergeant (E-8) in the 1/19th Special Forces Group (Airborne) Utah Army National Guard, just returned from Afghanistan. He spoke of his experiences. By then, the fire has burned down and is smoldering....

The color of the crowd literally changes when the announcer calls "All scouts report to portal H." Before that announcement is made, the stadium is filled with a constantly moving, multicolored, pulsing, living, breathing, disconnected crowd of people of all ages and genders. But when that announcement is made, there is a moment of silence. Then figures in the scout colors of navy, green and *brown begin to take a shape of their own and all move as one in the same direction, all heading for portal H. They are scouts. Cub Scouts, Boy Scouts, Girl Scouts and Brownie Scouts. It is truly amazing. Before the announcement, you never would have realized there were that many scouts in the audience! The final flag to be placed on the smoldering fire is the large flag from the Spanish Fork arena. Then the new huge flag is raised to the national anthem and everyone faces the new flag and repeats the Pledge of Allegiance. Just try to experience this without coming away with a new patriotic love of country!*

These events would have made B. Davis Evans so happy! What a town!

FARM IRRIGATION
by B. Davis Evans; March 28, 1968

Dear Reader;

…When I was very young, my father bought stock in the Strawberry Water Project and we began irrigating 140 acres of our 160-acre dry farm. Much of the terrain was side hill, some level and parts of it later became a good gravel pit. The streams were medium sized due to control on side-hill watering. An irrigation turn of 200 hours every two weeks or so was common place all summer long and what's more the ranch was near the mouth of Spanish Fork Canyon where Old C.W. (canyon wind) never failed.

But the irrigating turn I hated most was the April turn. The company would issue free water because of the early run off and naturally we took our share. Very few places on the ranch could the water be left running over two hours. So he who watered caught his sleep in spurts of two hour periods. So we slept on the ditch bank, our trusty alarm clock clanged us awake and we ventured forth to move the damn dam.

When I see a farmer today equipped with beautiful cement head-gates, I have a feeling I was born 30 years too soon. Our head-gates consisted of a long pole, a buggy wheel and a canvas dam, two sets, which we kept rotating down an 80 rod ditch. Some day try putting a long pole on one shoulder, a buggy wheel on the other, drag a large wet dam in one hand, get a shovel on there somewhere, then you'll get the picture.

One early spring morning, I lay at the bottom of a side-hill, newly planted in young lucern, waiting for the water to get to me. I decided to catch 40 winks so I put my hand out in the direction of the ditch, thinking that when the water touched it, I would awaken. Clad in miserable rubber boots, bib overalls and sheepskin lined coat, I fell asleep. The water double crossed me. It missed my hand and came onto me on each side and what awakened me was a wet, cold navel.

I jumped to my feet as the ice cold water ran into my boots. The sheepskin coat was dripping wet. I stood there in that pre-dawn canyon breeze, shrieking a curse to the sky (I stole that line from a poem, "the Highwayman").

But regardless of my misery I had to stay with the water. One didn't waste water even though it was free. About two hours later my brother came to relieve me and I hurried home to get into a good warm bath and to this day the bath tub is to me the most valuable thing in my home. It is still the "pause that refreshes" such as it did during my ranching days of the 30s and 40's…

The above experience is only one of many that haunted me during the years of my teens and beyond. It's another story of introducing water to a land that was less valuable than water.…

P.S. - I still sleep in two hour spurts.

City water turns were different. The irrigation water joyfully gurgled down the streets in gutters approximately 12" wide. The mud in the bottom was usually dark and soft. As a city girl, when I would come to town to visit my grandma, I would sit for hours with my feet in the ditch while I read a book. I squished my toes in the glorious soft mud. Now, this was up on the bench.

My other grandma lived in the "Silk Stocking" area of town on a farm. That was a totally different type of water turn. The water originated in the big ditch out of the millrace. It flooded the pasture and garden. At the end of the turn the water flooded the front lawn. Oh! How we loved to go out and splash in the water! It was about two inches deep and we could run and slide in the water and just get soaked! We loved it. Grandma, not so much.

The water also ran in a concrete ditch down the west side of Main Street on certain days. Children were not allowed to sit in the gutter and there wasn't much soft mud to squish your feet in. But that didn't stop the young ones from sailing a boat from one street corner down the block while running alongside and snatching it up right before it went into the culvert under the road, then trotting back up to the corner and sending the little boat (or rubber shoe) down again and again. What fun!

We also had twig races. Each child had to choose the perfect twig and break it off a nearby bush. The competition was brutal. If you chose the fastest twig you had to grab it before it went under the road or you would have to forfeit. The smartest contender had to be the one who chose a twig just a tiny bit slower, to be the fastest runner who was sure enough on his feet to grab the twig at the last second! It was cut-throat competition!

The irrigation ditches ran in a beautiful crisscross pattern all over town making it possible for the townspeople to irrigate their summer gardens, flower patches and front lawns all summer long, both night and day. And pity the man who stole someone's water turn!

The irrigation ditches ended at the North end of town on Ed Clark's property, south of the Allen Thomas' trailer court that is now the North Park Splash Pad. First it was just a swampy, muddy catch pond that some years went dry and other years was a mosquito ridden mushy mess. Then, the city fathers made a ball park, sand volleyball court (which was a disaster for a city with as much wind as we have here), a playground, picnic pavilion, and walking trail. The new post office was built across the street and now it is surrounded with Costco, Maceys, etc.

CAN'T PROGRESS WITHOUT CHANGE
by B. Davis Evans; November 30, 1967

Dear Reader:

Many changes have taken place in our town since I was a kid. These changes are all part of the progress of civilization, but with them much of the romance that was once part of a kid's life has gone. Mom and Dad, don't you remember only a decade or so ago when the old coal-burning engines that furnished the power to pull the trains along the tracks on the east and west sides of our town roared by, and nearly every kid in town had a desire to go and see them.

I wonder how many thousands of kids have stood on the "cut" bridge east of town and thrilled as a puffing, snorting monster has rumbled beneath them.

These engines had a mournful whistle, a clanging bell and steam and smoke poured out into the air, making a small boy feel as though all the magic and power in the world were mixed up in them.

He looked upon the men who manned them as heroes. He wanted to be like them, when he became a man, and travel to faraway places beyond the hills of our valley.

I haven't heard a small boy in years express the desire to be a train engineer. These modern diesels don't make enough noise and they are built in such a way that one can't tell where the engine ends and the train begins.

Another steam monster that's impossible for me to forget is the old steam engine that furnished the power to run the threshing machines. They screamed and puffed and crushed the rocks on the gravel roads as they slowly made their way from farm to farm or from city lot to city lot as many farmers did their threshing here in the city so as to put the grain near their granaries and the straw nearer their animals that were then allowed to live in town with us.

Ah, what a joy for a small boy to watch these big awkward threshing combinations set up. Generally the steam engine would be out in the street and the separator would be hidden back among the grain stacks on the lot. A great belt about 100 feet long, give or take a few feet, connected the engine with the threshing machine (I suppose the engine was far away so as not to set fire to the grain). Anyway, it took two or three strong men to put the belt on the big fly wheel and then onto a smaller wheel of the separator. The puffing steam monster backed up a little, the belt became taut and all was ready. The engineer threw the fly wheel in gear, there was a slipping and slapping sound as the belt and the separator trembled in a convulsive way as its innards started grinding and blowing and soon she was hungrily easting up the bundles of grain as the men atop the grain stacks tossed bundles into her hopper.

Those men who controlled these monsters were great in the eyes of little boys who watched from a distance and vowed that they would run threshing machines when they grew to be men.

The machine is gone. A steam engine is a museum piece and a few grain separators dot our countryside, slowly rusting away. They have given way to the combines. Little boys in town now don't know when the grain harvest is on anymore. The day was when, on a late summer day we would stand outside and listen for the sound of that monster somewhere in town, and when we heard it, away we'd go in that direction. It was something like the sound of the Pied Piper's flute.

A custom that was observed very religiously in those days was the feeding of the workmen who assisted with the threshing. This activity brought the women fold in on the job. I can remember my mother getting ready for the threshers for days before. She cooked two or three types of meat, mashed a bushel of potatoes, made a gallon or two of gravy, etc., etc., etc. She fed them homemade ice cream and pie for dessert. We hauled the food to the ranch in a buggy. She spread tablecloths on the ground in the shade of a grain stack and when high noon came, about 16 dirty, hungry men gobbled down the food. When the harvest was big this went on for two, even three days—I loved it. It was more important to me than Thanksgiving.

After the meal and a short rest, those heavily fed men had to go back to work. I often wondered how they made it. At one o'clock the engine tooted its whistle, belched a cloud of black smoke into the air, the belt slapped and the separator shook and then Geslie Bearnson, whose outfit always threshed our grain and who probably has directed more grain threshing than any man in the valley, would call out above the din of the machines: "White men on the stack; Icelanders in the straw." I was not sure what he meant; all those dirty men looked alike to me.

Yes, the steam engines are gone from our farms, our tracks and I guess from our waterways, but the memory of them still remain with this lad.

Certainly progress has brought change. The thresher engines are gone and the grain fields have been replaced with cul-de-sacs and soccer fields. Moms don't cook all day for the workers. They just make a quick stop at Costco on their way home from work. When they arrive home, they reload all the children and head for the pavilion at the soccer field. Once there, they unload all the children, food and stacks of paper plates, cups, plastic utensils and water bottles. Everyone has a quick, quiet dinner gathered along the picnic tables that are secured to the concrete floor. Dinner is quiet because everyone is texting or playing games on their phones. When the meal is finished, the moms gather the paper and plastic remains and shoves them in one of many trash cans, gathers the children and loads them into the van and returns them home again. Who works harder—the new moms or the moms from the steam engine days?

Very few little boys want to run threshing machines when they grow up. Instead, they want to play football or baseball professionally or become bankers or teachers.

Once there were two young men working on the construction of a new home being built in a new subdivision. One was a university student of home construction, the other a professional heavy equipment operator with no university training. The college student used his hand-held little computer to figure the proper elevation for the drain line. The other young man figured it out in his head from previous experience. They both came up with the same numbers. The professional operator laughed good-naturedly and said he had attended "the school of hard knocks."

A Freeway Comes To Spanish Fork
by B. Davis Evans; November 16, 1967

Dear Reader:

…The freeway has come to town. We now have nearly all the things that big cities have; swimming pool, golf course, a library, a stage second to none, etc., etc., etc. And now a freeway runs right by our town. Soon the traffic will be cut loose on it and 13 Service stations (give or take a couple either way) along our business loop will be bypassed. Progress is a wonderful thing but sometimes it is difficult to take on the chin especially in this case and especially if one happens to be a service station owner.

I was soured on freeways long before the first one ever came to Utah. We were motoring happily along near Riverside, California on a new freeway. I drove on the far right side desiring to keep away from speeders. Suddenly an exit was upon me and all the cars in my lane were taking it so I took it too. I knew not where I was going but I was certainly on my way at about 60 miles an hour. Out in the toolies I slowed down and found a place where I could turn around, but as my luck would have it, some "old duffer" was selling cement animals of all kinds from his front lawn and there I was in his driveway. "Oh! Look!" cried Virginia. "Cement ducks, skunks, frogs, squirrels, and all those lovely animals that I've always wanted!" "It's too far to haul that junk, Mother dear," said I.

"We can fill the trunk and we'll never know we have them," said she.

"I need all the money I have to get us to where we're going."

I moaned.

"We'll skimp a little here and there; after all you didn't buy a very big engagement ring. I think you can buy me a skunk or two."

We left that place about an hour later. The rear end of that car was so low that it was hard for me to see over the front end and as we traveled, one would swear we had no springs or shock absorbers.

Anyway, we carried that cement load to Mexico and back. We still have one skunk and one squirrel from that load. They stand in my garden as monuments to *A Freeway Mistake*. I have never made an exit mistake on a freeway since.

A few years ago, we decided to go to Disneyland on our vacation. All went well until we arrived at those confusing freeways that are everywhere in the vicinity of Los Angles. I saw the Matterhorn of Disneyland protruding out of the smog, but I couldn't find an exit to take me there. I finally took a frontage road and found a farmer leaning on his hoe in a patch of beans and I put the question to him: "How do I get there?"

He pondered for a moment and said, "Well, you know that exit you took? I wouldn't go back that way if I were you." "Thank you. I won't." I had the feeling that guy was about as stupid as I was.

"You go down here a couple of miles; no, you go west from here; no, you…well son, I don't think you can get to Disneyland from here."

Yes, progress is a wonderful thing, but when it comes someone must adjust.

When you hear someone reminisce about "dragging Main" this refers to sometime before 1968, and before the freeway. Main Street entered town from Salem and went north to 800 North. A traveler on his way to Provo would then turn right off Main and head east until the road curved to the north and headed to Springville and on into Provo. At the north end of Spanish Fork Main Street, the road did a huge U-turn and headed back south. On the west side of Main Street at the U-turn there was the Arch Movie Theater, which was a large Quonset-type metal building and the Frostop. Later on that corner of 8th North and Main after the movie house went down, the city built a police station which is now the Parks and Recreation Building. If you ever have the occasion to enter that building from the back, go down the outside stairs and try to imagine a prisoner in shackles navigating those stairs!

Here's a game: Name all the gas stations/service stations you can remember and place them around town as you recall. Then compare your results with an old friend.

BECOME WHAT YOU DREAM
by B. Davis Evans; date unknown

Dear Reader:

A Few years ago I stood on the corner of 87th Street and Broadway in New York City and looked up toward the top of the Empire State Building. All but about 20 stories of her top were shrouded in clouds. The thought came to me, "The plan for this building was born in the minds of some man, a man who probably looked like thousands of other men, but something was hidden from view to him; that something was a dream, a drive to accomplish something that no other man had ever accomplished. The other, hidden something within him was his ability to see his dream through to its completion!

These same thoughts come to me as I travel over the Oakland Bay Bridge, or ride through the tunnels under the Hudson, or behold the massive network of freeway that carry our traffic above, beneath, and through our cities, or the beauty in the paintings and sculpture work at Forrest Lawn, or the magnificent architecture of our own Salt Lake Temple, accomplished with only the crude tools of our pioneer craftsmen or the myriad things too numerous to mention that cause me to stand in awe as I think of the works of my fellow man and I am reminded of David's Psalms:

"O Lord, what is man that thou art mindful of him? For thou has made him a little lower than the angels, and thou has crowned him with glory and honor. Thou madest him to have dominion over the works of thy hands"

And what has this to do with our town, you might ask. It has this; we are living in a time when we have access to all the wonder of the world whether we become acquainted with them by travel, by pictures or through our reading. Our town can be as broad as the whole world.

The official date when B. Davis Evans wrote this article is unknown. It could have been approximately 1967. He mentioned mans ability to see wonders and then create his own. He referenced how we have the ability, availability, the imagination and innovation. Oh what wonders we can create! Just think how much Spanish Fork has accomplished since 1967.

Chapter 3:
Who We Are

The Question Was Asked: "What makes the people of Spanish Fork love this town so much?"

To begin with, there was a diverse bunch of immigrants from different parts of Europe who spoke different languages, had different cultures and traditions but had given up absolutely everything to come to America and eventually Utah. They all traveled the same direction and ended up in the same place. They set up camp and eventually staked out a piece of the wilderness close together, seeking safety for themselves and for each other. Although they clung to their own kin, they shared a basic philosophy with each family. This is where they chose to end their journey. With very little disparity, they helped and protected one another as they began their adventure as neighbors.

As such, their families grew, multiplied, and even intermarried. The families today still cling to some small segment of their origins. However, even now, they are still helping each other with projects, sharing their skills and talents in order to create a better place.

Even before this piece of wilderness became an official town the residents were helping each other any way they could. They helped each other plow and plant crops. If a husband was working in the mines up at Thistle, for example, someone would see that his stock was sheltered and fed and then check on the wife and children. As the population grew the dynamics changed a little. The men had their own bunch of friends. They even referred to them positively as "their gang." If one fellow's tractor threw a fan belt, one of his gang would come up with a remedy in the crisis. The men would congregate, usually at the barbershop, to discuss and solve the problems of the day, be it the weather or the wife, the crops or the kids.

The women always found time to get together to help each other on big projects. Sometimes they would even create the project as an excuse for the time together. Thus began the infamous "club." There are women living in Spanish Fork today who have been members together in the same club for over fifty years. They have put on programs, put up fruit, and put together quilts. The women of this community have raised crops, raised children, raised pennies by the inch for a justified cause, and if necessary, raised a ruckus for a good reason.

As times changed, the gangs became service clubs. The men didn't change, only the name of the gang. The men would sometimes think of a nice event and invite their wives. Better yet, they would suggest to the wife, "Honey, the Kiwanis thought it might be nice to have some kinda shindig in February and invite the wives, but we don't know how to go about it. What do you think?" And the party was planned, food prepared, tables decorated, dresses made, dishes gathered. Everyone took part and had a great time. The change from a group of just buddies to a service club was like magic to this town.

One example is The Diamond Fork Riding Club. To belong to that club you should have a horse. You also need a sponsor, a member of the club, to recommend you to the group. These guys really made the first rodeos happen. Some members either worked at or had friends who worked at the pipe plant who donated pipes to make the bucking shoots. Somebody provided the perfect dirt for the arena. One guy who had an available tractor would level it out and another would rake it. The members of the club would practice their serpentine maneuvers twice a week before the rodeo. At first the members of the club would create the programs for the rodeo and hand them out. For years, the crowd cheered the club members on their "trailer race." Everyone knew who would probably fall off his horse or who would win, but we yelled and laughed each time as if it were the first. Everyone also knew that Ron Davis was the best leader of the riding club's drill team.

The men were having such a great experience that the wives also wanted a riding club of their own. So the Saddle Dusters began. These women could raise kids, husbands *and* ride horses while looking terrific. The groups would combine sometimes and go on special rides. They sometimes had a breakfast ride where between fifteen and twenty riders would pack up early in the morning and ride up a favourite canyon, breathing in the crisp, clean mountain air. Then they would stop in the designated spot and sit together and share breakfast. After breakfast just as the air began to warm up, they would clean up, pack it all up and ride back down the beautiful canyon.

A favorite ride for the riding club was the family ride, where the guys could ride just a few miles from town with their kids and without the wives and mothers! The plan was not to go so far from town that any "emergency" could not be readily handled. The kids would sit and talk about the ride for weeks and with each telling, the trip became longer and more dangerous. Sometimes the riding club would go to the desert to see and maybe chase wild horses. That excursion would last from a Wednesday into Sunday. Lately, they sometimes plan a pack trip into the Book Cliffs, Henri's Mountain or Boulder Mountain. Sometimes they have gone over the hills to Strawberry.

However, no matter where they go, or for how long they go, they make sure they are back to town in time for The Fiesta Days Rodeo. The guys in the club look forward to Fiesta Days every year as they have since about 1945, when the LDS Church suggested that every city should set aside a time to have a celebration of their hometown. Except, of course, according to them, Spanish Fork's celebration is always one of a kind and the "best of the bunch!" Then, at the end of the festivities as the dust settles in the beautiful arena and the grass at the city office and the city park starts to regain its green color, the Diamond Fork Riding Club has a "Thank Goodness the Rodeo is Over" party!

Another gang in town started a service club called the Jaycees. This club was comprised of some of the great city leaders. It didn't matter if they held public office or not, these men volunteered their time to many worthy projects. It was the Jaycees who put on the first Easter egg hunts. They used real eggs, hard boiled the eggs and then wrote a name of a merchant who would give the finder a prize. It was a great marketing tool because the parent had to take the children to each store to receive the nickel, dime, or treat (Apparently, this was before the time when anyone worried about eating hard boiled eggs that sat in the egg cartons until the marker dried, lay on the tall grass on the ball field until the hunt began and then had been rolling around on the backseat of the car for hours).

There used to be a city baseball field on the corner of Center Street between 600 East and 700 East. It was called the "East Bench City Square." Nebo School District decided to buy the baseball field and build a new school there on the whole square block. That is where the Park School got its name. However, this caused some concern among the townspeople because each city had its own baseball team. So, the team needed a ball field. The baseball field on East Center was a Semi-pro field. So, of course, the Jaycees, to name a few—Norm Barnes, the Nelson brothers, Bill, Mark and Wayne, Howard Creer, Allen Evans—and many volunteers got together with the city and built a new ball field on the other side of town. With help from friends like Bill Peery, they built the light towers. Then, each year the Jaycees would plan a project in the spring to repair, or paint the bleachers. They would care for the fields, trim the grass and do anything necessary to beautify their baseball field. The Kiwanis Club got into the act also. Even when The Lions Club was functioning, they adopted a field and cared for it. So, you will notice today, a Jaycee Field and a Kiwanis Field down at the Russell Swenson Ballpark on 300 South and 300 West.

Now, many of you may wonder why it is called The Russell Swenson Ball Park? Jack and DeAnn Swenson had 4 children. Russell was their youngest son. He was born in 1961 and he was born with Down's syndrome. This was the generation that did not discuss conditions like Down's syndrome. Except, courageous parents like Jack and DeAnn did discuss it with each other. They decided to raise their son just like they had raised all of their children. Jack began his work career in 1952 when, as a sophomore, his job was to sweep the high school gym floor. By 1970 he went from working for Rulon Thomas part time as the swimming pool supervisor to being the city Parks and Recreation Director. As director, Jack was involved with all city-sponsored sports including basketball and baseball. So, he took Russell with him on all his excursions to check on the baseball fields, basketball courts and the pristine condition of the many city parks.

As Russell grew up, he was encouraged to play any sport his heart desired. With the support of his brothers, Russell not only played on the teams but he was an assistant groundskeeper. He even had one special lawnmower that he claimed. Everyone on the grounds crew knew that they did not touch Russell's mower! In addition to playing the different games, Russell was an avid fan. He happily cheered on his favourite teams and was an excellent example of good sportsmanship to all. Over time, there were hundreds of boys and girls who watched and learned as Russell played his hardest every time. Sometimes, from the stands, as a strikeout batter with head hung down slumped into the dugout, he would hear Russell shout, "Good try!"

That's why, when the city built the new baseball complex and retired the old ballpark, it was renamed The Russell Swenson Ballpark and the Jaycees and Kiwanis fields remain. Children still play on those fields and parents still gather there to cheer on their young players.

CHURCH

In *The History of Spanish Fork* by Elisha Warner, page 33 we were all told about the origin of the Church of Jesus Christ of Latter-day Saints in Spanish Fork. This is a wonderful, concise description and timetable. It lists the names of the strong families that willingly sacrificed their time and talent in the building of this community. As you read it, you will recognize the names of the families that still reside in Spanish Fork. Just to paraphrase; the Spanish Fork Branch was organized in March of 1851.

"In 1865, Bishop Thurber was called on a mission to England. During this absence, President Brigham Young came to visit the saints in Spanish Fork. A meeting was called and Bishop Aaron Johnson of Springville became Bishop of Spanish Fork as well as Springville. This arrangement was not entirely satisfactory to the Spanish Fork saints. They did not like the idea of paying their tithing to a Springville bishop. Tithing, at that time, consisted of a part of everything they had...vegetables, butter, eggs, pork, flour, wheat, and molasses were all on the tithing list. The people of Spanish fork figured these articles should be used by the needy of their town, not by the needy of Springville.

"To help the situation, George W. Wilkins was appointed to act as President of the Spanish Fork Ward with William Robertson tithing clerk. They were instructed to have certain articles of tithing sent to the Springville bishop.

The people of Spanish Fork did not pay their tithing as they should, not being wholly converted to this arrangement, but Bishop Johnson continued to hold a certain jurisdiction over Spanish Fork until January 1867, when

Bishop Thurber returned home from his mission to Europe. He again took charge of the Spanish Fork Ward, and the Saints were given the privilege of paying their tithing to their Bishop in their town.

"At a ward conference held in the Central Meeting House on December 20, 1891, Spanish Fork was divided into four wards, namely, First, Second, Third, and Fourth. The boundaries established were; First East and Second North Streets. The First Ward was the Southeast part of the city, Second ward in the Southwest, Third Ward in the Northwest and Fourth Ward in the Northeast."

First Ward Church

From this simple beginning in 1851, one LDS ward has now become six stakes with dozens of wards just in Spanish Fork, Palmyra and Benjamin.

There was also a Lutheran church on Center Street and 1000 East. The Icelanders had their own church where only Icelandic was spoken where some of the early Icelanders attended. As the Icelanders became more familiar with the English language they worshiped with the LDS Church. In later years, the Lutherans went to church services in Provo. We should not assume that every person living in Spanish Fork was (or is) LDS.

Faith Baptist Church

Hari Krishna Temple

There are several different faiths in Spanish Fork and the surrounding area. Hari Krishna, 7th Day Adventists, Catholics, Baptists, agnostics, antagonists and just plain sluffers!

———————————

Recently in our neighborhood, a young man coined a phrase: "Churchly things." The phrase was very well received and the neighbors now smile and use the phrase, or modify it to fit the moment. Perhaps they would say, "Bishoply things," or "Deaconly things."

In Spanish Fork and the surrounding areas, the people or especially "The Mormons" do a lot of "churchly things" all week but especially on Sunday. Because of school, sports, and multiple jobs for parents, "churchly things" are scheduled for some evenings and then bunched together on Sunday. Now, we both lounge around all morning and then rush to get cleaned up and to our Church meeting block of three hours on time. Then we rush back home, throw a big meal together, eat, clean it up, and then spend some time scheduling the upcoming week. Or, we jump out of bed, rush to church, rush home and check the Crockpot, then dive under the covers for a sweet Sunday nap, followed by the requisite Crockpot meal, complete with Jell-O that was prepared on Saturday. Obviously, I'm generalizing—not everyone eats Jell-O. I've even heard that people of all religions eat Jell-O, even people who never do "churchly things."

All kidding aside, back in the day, Sunday morning breakfast in many families was a sweet roll and a cup of juice followed by dressing in our Sunday clothes. I had Sunday shoes, and if it was a good year, I could choose one of my two Sunday dresses. After my mother finished braiding our hair, and straightening everyone's bows and socks, we were loaded into the car for the ride to our church. Upon arriving, we all were supposed to walk quietly to the big singing room at the back of the church that was just for kids. There were some mothers there too, one on each row. We would sing and sing! And hear stories about Jesus. Then we would march quietly to one of several small classrooms down the hall.

Once inside the small classroom, there were little chairs to sit on that were just perfect. My feet could touch the floor! Our teacher told some more great stories about how to be kind and not fight with our sisters, no matter what. She always had great big pictures that she could hang on the chalkboard from the very top. When she was finished with us she sent us out into the hallway to find our parents quietly. When our family was all rounded up, we piled back into the car and went home again.

As soon as we got home, we changed out of our Sunday clothes into play clothes while Mother fixed a great big dinner. It was always bigger than the dinners during the week. She always put the pickles and olives out in the special dishes with little forks by the dish. As soon as dinner was over and the dishes were done, I would go into the living room and Daddy would read the funnies to me. Then I would go to my room and play dolls for awhile so my mother could take a nap.

When she woke up, it was time to get dressed up again in my Sunday clothes and back to church we went. This time we all sat together in the big carpeted room. While an old person talked, we were expected to sit quietly, but not really required to listen. We could draw pictures as long as we didn't rustle the papers. My sisters liked to make those things you make by folding the paper a million different ways and then write secret messages on each corner, and then pinch the different corners together to see the messages. Sometimes, my Mother would let me play with her hands and push the blue-gray veins on the top of her hand to see it move all around. That would keep me quiet for a good ten minutes. Sometimes, I wished that I had a crying baby that I could take upstairs to the balcony room that looked over the big room. Sitting up there would be so fun! I could see the top of everyone's head. And If I had a real crying baby, I could sing to her without anyone hearing me. After more singing and talking, we were done and could then go home for good until next week.

Sometimes, when we got home, my sisters would go downtown to the movie, or even to The Paramount in Provo (usually with boys). Sometimes, my friend and I would trade families for the day. I would go home from morning church with her. I would change into her play clothes, eat dinner with her family, and then we would go downstairs into her basement and build a super tent using the ping-pong table, any available chairs and lots of blankets draped all around. Then we would crawl in and play house or detective or something. When her mother called down the stairs, we would rush up, change back into our Sunday clothes and go back to church. My friend and I traded families as often as our parents allowed.

When our family finally got home again, we would set up the TV trays and watch Bonanza while we ate a tuna fish sandwich with a bowl of bottled peaches. What a day!

We also had church during the week. There were meetings for just the moms on Tuesday morning, teenagers Tuesday night, and regular kids on Wednesday after school. The kids who lived in Lakeshore had it easy on Wednesdays because their school was just across the street from the church. So when their school teacher was finished with them for the day, she just sent them out the door and across the road to the church. When they got to the church (sometimes, they just *had* to check out the back parking lot first), their "churchly" teacher had after-school treats for them first. This was a good thing because they were starving!

LDS Seminary Building

No matter if you lived in Leland, Palmyra, Lakeshore or in town, Primary was basically the same. They went to the big room and had to find their row which was marked with a special flag for each class. One girl found out the hard way that the row with the flag that had a hatchet on it was just for boys. Once they were all quiet (it was the Big Room, so you had to be quiet) the lady in charge would talk to them for a few minutes, they would sing Happy Birthday to whoever had gotten older, and then time for some more singing. Then they would all quietly march out of the big room row by row and go to their own classroom for some more stories and "churchly" stuff. By the time Primary was over, the moms were there to pick up the kids and take them home.

Some evenings and even some Saturdays, the bigger boys could play basketball in the church rec hall. The boys had special shorts with matching shirts. There were some even bigger boys who wore black pants and zebra-striped shirts that would run around the room and blow on whistles. The boys and men seemed to know what the rules were, even though sometimes they yelled at one another a lot. I heard that sometimes on Saturdays, if there were no games, some boys would show up and play a game or two and then sneak into the custodian's office, where he kept all the brooms, cleaning stuff and a secret cold pop machine. It was the kind of machine that held pop bottles that could be slid down to the end and pulled out after the money was put into the machine slot. However, those boys figured out that if they brought their own long straws, they could just pop off the bottle cap, stick the straw right into the cold bottle of pop and get themselves a nice cold drink!

GROWING UP IN SPANISH FORK
by Lori Bradford Barber; October 8, 2015

I was born in Spanish Fork in 1963 at the little Hughes Hospital on the West side of town. That building was converted into apartments years ago, and many people don't know that Spanish Fork ever had a hospital. Dr. Wells Brockbank delivered me and also took out my tonsils at the age of five in that same hospital.

I spent the majority of my first 11 years growing up on South Main Street in a house that used to sit about where "The Dugout" is located. That stretch of road was called Bradford Lane because there were so many Bradfords living there. To this day, there are still some Bradfords living on Bradford Lane.

I loved my childhood growing up in Spanish Fork. I always wished my children could have had the experience of growing up in a small town and living on a farm as I did. Spanish Fork had grown so much by the time I had children that it seemed like a completely different place from the one in which I was raised. As a young girl, my family seemed to know nearly everyone in town, and we were probably related to most of them.

My dad, Glen Bradford, ran a large sheep farm with his father, Mark Bradford, and other relatives and employees. I remember the stock barns and auctions that were held on Saturdays in buildings near the rodeo grounds. Most of those buildings have been torn down. As a young girl, it was my job to get the tickets from the auctioneer after livestock at been sold and run them to the business office. I had to climb over the fences and shoots where the livestock were being held and I was scared to death that I would fall and get trampled by those animals. I did love the sound of the auctioneer's voice. To this day when I hear an auctioneer, it reminds me of the stock barns and auctions.

Just north of the buildings was a swampy area where we would ice skate in the winter and catch tadpoles in the summer. The canal just north of that area was also a favorite place to swim and play. There was a large water pipe for that canal going under the road near the entrance to the river bottoms. We would climb into the water pipe and let the water shoot us out on the other side. That was so much fun! I'm quite sure our parents didn't know half of the things we did as we were growing up or we might not have lived to tell about it.

Our farm was where the newer ballpark now stands. The old white house remaining on the corner just south of The Dugout was built by my great-grandparents. My great-grandfather and his brother homesteaded that area and much of the land that was behind that home, which includes the land where all of the ball fields, soccer fields, tennis courts, and homes west of the Spanish Fork River now sit, and including the land behind The Dugout.

I have many fond memories of playing out in the fields and down by the Spanish Fork River. They were great times. We were free to do nearly anything we wanted outdoors and were not bound by technology or the fear that someone was going to kidnap us. We would head outdoors in the morning and often not come back until the sun started to set. It was a great time to be a kid.

My sisters, friends and I used to walk to Al's Market several times a week to buy penny candy. If we had 5 cents, we could get a candy bar. Beef jerky was a real treat but the "good kind" was expensive (15 cents) and we rarely had enough money for that. Allen Warner owned that small grocery store, located on the south end of Main Street. It wasn't very far from my home. Allen was a cheerful, friendly man and always had a smile on his face. I remember hearing him whistling often. He was really good at it. He would whistle along with music or without. I remember him whistling to music at ward parties.

Allen died fairly young and Al's Market was never the same. He also had a daughter, Lisa, who was best friends with my big sister, LeeAnn. Lisa was diagnosed with diabetes as a young teenager and died within a year of her father dying. Her death was one of the first deaths that had a big impact on me.

Lisa used to sneak candy out of her dad's store and occasionally bring it to my sister and me. One of her jobs at the store was "doing bottles." This meant that when people would come to the store to buy soda, they would bring their used glass bottles in a small carrier, and the cost of their new ones would be less if they returned their empty bottles. Lisa's job was sorting the bottles in the dark, scary basement of Al's Market. The basement wasn't really a basement. It was just on open, dirt area underneath the back of the store that had been dug out a little in order to store the bottles. We often helped her sort the bottles so she would be able to play with us sooner.

The friends we used to hang around with in the neighbourhood were the Warner kids, Gardners, Bradfords, Jex's, and Barretts. The kids that were closer to mine and my sister's age got together often to play night games. Sometimes we would sneak out of our homes at night and meet outside to play truth or dare or go on some big adventure like going to the vacant house behind the Jex's (which has been torn down since), as it was surely haunted. Most often we would end up scaring ourselves to death by hearing noises or seeing things in the dark that would freak us out and cause us to bolt towards our homes.

We thought we were very clever by never once getting caught sneaking out of the houses. Looking back now, as a parent myself, I realize that we weren't so clever after all. We had no idea of the potential danger we had put ourselves in, and worse was the fact that none of our parents had a clue we were even gone.

Growing up there were only four elementary schools in town. I went to the Thurber School, which is now the city office building. Park, Brockbank and Rees were the other elementary schools. The Rees School was rebuilt in a new location and is now just an old, run-down building. The other two schools are still functioning as elementary schools at the time of this writing. When Larsen Elementary was built, it seemed strange to have five elementary schools in town, and shortly after that they seemed to pop up everywhere.

My mom would take us to school in the mornings, and most often we walked home. On the sidewalks between Thurber and my home, and on many of the surrounding blocks, someone (a kid or group of kids, I'm guessing) marked an "X" in the cement every ten steps. I don't know why this was done, but it was fun for us watching for the X's and finding them at exactly ten steps. I suspect there might be some old sidewalks in town that still have some X's carved in them.

After elementary school, which was from kindergarten to fifth grade, we went to middle school for sixth and seventh grades. It was located on 100 North and the old Central School was part of the middle school. I believe the Central School was an elementary school before I was born.

Central School

The junior high was the "old high school" at the time I was in middle school, and it was located where the Nebo School District offices were. The gym is still intact and is preserved because of its historical significance. Junior high was for eighth and ninth graders. By the time I got to junior high school, the new "Middle School/Junior High Complex" had been built on the east side of town, just off of Canyon Road. My class got to help move the books, desks, etc. to the new school. It was exciting to go to a brand new school, but I was never able to attend school in the old junior high building.

High School Building

I remember that at lunch time, Glade's Drive-In was crazy busy with junior high kids coming from next door. My husband used to go there often for lunch. His usual order was "thirty-five fry, fifteen Coke." We used to order by the price of things that had sizes, rather than the size. So what he meant was he wanted the size of French fries that cost 15 cents and a ten-cent Coke.

For entertainment, my friends and I would ride our bicycles to the stores on Main Street and wander around, wishing we had more money to buy some of the cool things. Forseys, the Gift Fair, and the three drug stores (City, World and Stone Drug) were the stores we liked the most.

We would also go to movies at one of the two theaters in town—one in the middle of Main Street and one at the north end of town—I think it was named "Arches."

I remember kids bringing birds inside so they would fly around in front of the screen. The managers weren't happy about that but we sure thought it was funny, especially when we would see the managers getting so frustrated trying to catch the birds.

Arch Theater

Summer jobs for kids usually involved helping on someone's farm or picking cherries in nearby orchards. The boys would help haul hay, throwing those heavy bales on the back of wagons. Girls used to babysit a lot to earn money. I think I started out making 25 cents an hour to babysit. We were in a transition period of making versus buying clothes. As a young girl, my mom and grandma made most of my clothes. As I became a teenager, buying clothes was much more common.

"Rodding Main" was a favorite past-time for teenagers. We would drive from one end of Main to the other, "flipping U-ies" by Bob's (which is now Fast Gas) on the north end of town, and by Premium Oil, which is now torn down, but was located on the south end of town.

Spanish Fork was and is a great place to grow up. It has gotten so big that it is impossible to know people like we did when I was young. However, it still has that small town feel and to me, is the best place in the world to live.

WELCOME WAGON

There was a knock at the door. We had moved in last week, so there was not a bell installed yet. Maybe it was an "extra." We didn't care, there was no hurry. We were just so excited! This was our very own brand new first house. It even had bricks on the front. It didn't matter that all the houses looked alike. Well, almost alike. They were different colors and there were a couple of different floor plans in the neighborhood. But that was some of the excitement. All of us were in the basic same position. We finally had a neighborhood! We all had little children, student loans, old cars, hand-me-down furniture. We all cheered each other on. Each person's success was everyone's step up. Our children could run outside and play. The street was not busy. Who knows? In five years everyone will have some kind of fence. If somebody in town is contemplating a new fence and needed ideas, they could just ride around our neighborhood for lots of suggestions!

Today, at the door was a young women who was about my age, and pregnant too! But what I liked best was that she had brought me a dozen glazed donuts from the new grocery store! Yeah! Donuts! She was "The Welcome Wagon Lady." She gave me some coupons and trinkets from the local stores and encouraged me to shop in town. I learned who was teaching piano and dancing. I even learned that there is a clogging dance class upstairs in the firehouse! She had all the school schedules and told me how and where to sign up. She had information from the city office about our correct voting district, where to go to pay the city bill and she even directed me to the little house by the city park where I pay my gas bill (I would have missed that for sure).

Then she explained the yearly schedule. It took her a while because it was quite extensive. But I would have been lost without this information. I mean, my children would never succeed in this town if they didn't adhere to the schedule. It went like this:

JANUARY: clean up all Christmas decorations inside and outside of the house. Re-organize closets and cupboards.

FEBRUARY: make plans to attend the home show in St. George. If possible stay with friends or relatives who live in town until your children are in school. Then make motel reservations in the right motels way in advance. By attending the home show, you will know what will be trending that year in home décor. For instance, one year the correct color scheme for young female children was lime green carpet with yellow, pink and/ or orange. Why, on one street alone this array of colors was done in approximately five different ways including new curtains, matching bedspreads and darling ceramics!

Baseball starts in the Spring with pre-tournament games. As a rule, all parents, or at least one, attends every game, even if they have multiple games. The Welcome Wagon Lady had all the ballgame schedules.

Decorate your house, inside and out for valentines. Help your children make an extravagant valentine box to take to school as well as darling valentines and valentine treats for everyone. Also prepare valentines for all the neighbors. Then the children can go door to door with a parent and load up on candy. Yippee!

MARCH: finalize plans to go to St. George again for the Sunshine Baseball tournament. Spanish Fork is a huge baseball town. It is very important to go. It is also really fun. Everyone from Spanish Fork is down there and it is fun to ride up and down St. George Boulevard and see where everyone is staying. Then you just pull into a spot by your friends and your kids can swim and play for awhile between games.

In March don't forget Easter plans. Spanish Fork's Easter Egg Hunt is the biggest and best in the county. There are other, smaller hunts in other cities, but Spanish Fork's has the fire truck there to set off the hunt. One year, the poor fireman blew the fire whistle two seconds early! Pandemonium reigned. The fields weren't quite ready. The volunteers and parents weren't ready. What a riot! The poor guy felt terrible. Kids were crying.

March also has Spring festivals, piano recitals and dance recitals. Be prepared with at least an Easter outfit for each child and preferably one for yourself. I'm doing the math in my head… *cha ching! $$$*

APRIL: school will be out for a week sometime this month.
Many families go to Disneyland.

MAY: this is the winding down of the school year. There are track meets and especially the Hersey Track meet. For older children there is High School graduation.

JUNE: Spanish Fork City holds swimming lessons at the high school pool. Some of the classes are taught by the lifeguards from the city pool, so they must be excellent. One highlight of the lessons is that after the lesson is over the children hold their damp beach towels on their shoulders and run down the steep hill while screaming! This has a twofold benefit; it partially dries the swimming suit and also the towel so the towel won't stick to the vinyl seats in the car.

When they get home the children will most likely crash in front of the TV until time to change for baseball games. Games are held twice a week in the hottest time of day; 3 p.m.-5 p.m. Games are played in the baseball field just down the street from Glade's Drive-In (they call it a drive-in because that is exactly what you do— drive in to the edge of the building, run up to the window, order your hamburger, go back to your car and wait until they signal you that your order is ready. It's truly amazing! The girls working there never write your order down. They have to remember everything and they hardly ever get it wrong!).

Baseball practice is held at one of the ballparks around town; East Park by the junior high school, North Park field down by the trailer court, or Brockbank Elementary School.

JULY: July is the holiday month. The 4th of July Parade is held in Provo. It is a huge parade with bands and floats and some horses. You have to leave town early to get a good parking place and then walk to the parade route. On the evening of the 4th of July there is a huge firework show at the BYU football stadium. You pack blankets, lawn chairs, Kool- Aid, Rice Crispy treats, and all the kids in the car and go to Provo again (note: be sure to have everyone do a potty check before leaving home because it is a long evening). Moms are encouraged to tell soothing, quiet stories on the way home because the children will be hyper from all the fireworks and dads will be irritated by the horrendous traffic on the way home. Avoid cantankerous subjects in conversations.

Then there is the 24th of July. Now this is a real celebration! It runs for a week and begins with a cattle and horse parade, rodeos every night, the carnival in the middle of the street for days, hamburger stands on the city park and even breakfast in the park the day of the big parade. The day before the big parade is the Primary parade where all the children decorate their bikes or even have a float of their own! The winning float gets to be in the big parade on the 24th. It would be cool if the city would spring for fireworks! Oh well—maybe someday!

AUGUST: when the 24th of July celebrations are over, it is like the summer is over. All the stores have back-to-school sales. School starts in late August, so contact the schools and make sure that your children are registered in the right school, hopefully with the right teacher. Don't be silly, there is no "right" teacher. But there might be one who will put up with your children's shenanigans better than another!

The proper school clothes are Sears "tough skins" pants for the boys and t-shirts. The girls will need several colored long pants with interchangeable shirts. Red is always a safe, good color for either boys or girls and can be interchangeable.

August is a good time to harvest the garden that you planted after Mother's day. Pick all the nice tomatoes and peppers and squashes (this includes all the zucchini that you weren't able to give away to your unsuspecting neighbors). Shred the zucchini, pick the cucumbers, stew the tomatoes, mix the peppers, chilies, onions and tomatoes and make salsa. Make the zucchini into bread, freeze it to give to friends, family and teachers all year. *Warning: if you make sweet pickles, don't leave them in the only bathtub to soak because it will turn your bathtub green!

Take a breath, Welcome Wagon Lady!

SEPTEMBER: September is a lovely month! The children are back on schedule and in school most of the days. After school is a little hectic as you transport your children to and from school every day, then to and from Primary on Wednesday and to and from dance, piano, clogging, and singing the rest of the week. The weather is usually temperate so sweatshirts work in place of coats for the children.

OCTOBER: be prepared! October is a hectic, irregular month. There are several school vacation days, and UEA, which means Utah Education Association Convention. The Welcome Wagon Lady explained to me that she personally had never met anyone who actually attended the convention but it was a vacation from school as far as the children and parents were concerned. Except when the UEA meetings corresponded with the deer hunt! Then everyone only got one weekend vacation.

Now, deer hunt is an occasion, loved by many, and dreaded by the women. The men would hear the call of the wild. They planned the entire hunt right down to the wind direction. The women also planned. They planned meals, grocery lists, bedding, boots, socks, coats, hats, and of course, the orange vests. You couldn't forget the safety vests and bright orange sweatshirts because all the store clerks wore them during deer hunt season just to be part of the occasion. Some people were horrified to see a dead deer hanging from someone's front yard tree. But this was like a badge of honor, so others could stop by and ask for all the details of the hunt. The deer hunt was a toss-up in many marriages. Some women loved the outdoors, the constant smell of the bonfire, the camaraderie of the men. Some women loved the "man hunt food, woman cook for man." On the other hand some women would choose to go on a hunt of her own, with girlfriends at the mall.

Also in October, the Welcome Wagon Lady advised about Halloween. Each elementary school would have a huge Halloween party complete with a Sloppy Joe dinner, a spook house, cake walk, ring toss, and costume parade. This is 1975. All costumes are created at home. No fair buying one at Forseys.

November: the Welcome Wagon know-it-all woman who is now getting on my nerves said that the thing we should be the most thankful for, besides our family, is that it is only seven weeks until Christmas. "So, get going!" She gushed. Make several lists!" Those who get, those who give, those who should get—neighbors, school teachers, piano teachers, the milk man, the paper boy.

Then also make a list of your relatives, then your children and your husband. Include sizes on the children. Also make a list of who should get a Christmas card and separate it according to who should receive a handmade card and who will be alright with a store-bought card.

DECEMBER: because you were so totally organized last month, you only need to put your lists into action. All cards and gifts should be on their way out the door by the eleventh of December. I don't know who decided that day, but she said it. While you are shopping you might want to tuck in a gift for yourself in case your husband forgets.

Be sure to talk with your relatives and get the dates for the family Christmas party. Check with your husband's work for his office party date and time and food assignment. While you are downtown, stop into Forseys to pick up their special candy mix for the Christmas stockings—love that pink ribbon candy! *Special secret note: When you are in Forseys, make good friends with the "important" people and you just might get someone to get you one of the Cabbage Patch Dolls that are hidden in the special safe in the basement. If you are very good and very lucky!

When the holidays are all over be sure to check with Orr Electric and Stone Drug, or Zac's for any year-end sales.

By now, I had more than enough information from this woman. Before she could start in on some other important information that I must know, I practically pushed her out the door with a sincere promise to always shop in town.

This neighborhood was called "The Jex Subdivision." It was here that some great and powerful businesses began, and while working hand in hand, lasting friendships were formed—Bushman Press, Coach Roger Reed, Clark Swenson of Security Insurance, Peterson Accounting, and Neilsen Construction to name a few.

Whew! No wonder grandparents are so happy! They can just watch the parents do all this.

OH! TO BE EIGHT

The summer of 1958 was really hot in Utah! This is a pure fact in my eight-year-old brain, as related to me by my bare feet. The luscious smell of real bacon (from a pig, not the store) woke me up this morning. As soon as my eyes opened, I dropped out of bed, bare feet on the wonderfully cold, smooth basement floor, dug my glasses from one of the pockets hanging on the back of the bedroom door and made a run for the stairs. In the processes, I had to keep my eyes to the front so I would not look at the scary furnace. At the top of the stairs, once in the screen porch, I quietly crawled over my sisters asleep on the floor. It was definitely to my advantage not to wake them or else I would not make it into the bathroom first. The goal was to get in and out of the one bathroom before Grandpa. If I was too slow I would have to sneak outside to the side of the house and…you know.

Mother and Grammy were talking about nothing interesting as they prepared breakfast. I sat meekly at the table and innocently and quietly ate, hoping no one would notice that I had crawled over my sleeping sisters or dodged into the bathroom just two steps ahead of Grandpa—whew! My brother was making faces at me from the other side of the table and threatened to tell unless I gave him the last piece of bacon. He was always doing that. Like, at home, he would swing me from the banister and promise never to drop me. Then he would get me way out there, really high up where my feet couldn't touch and he'd let go of one hand and scare me to death! I gave him the piece of precious bacon. He always won.

After breakfast I disappeared back into the basement to get dressed until the dishes were done. Just as I returned to the top of the basement stairs, my brother and Grandpa passed by, headed out to the coop to work on some wood stuff. Mother and Grammy planed to set up a quilt and have some relatives over. I liked this because I could sit under the quilt and listen to all the secrets, although, sometimes I wasn't sure exactly what they were talking about.

So, it looked like a quiet day for me—either the quilting, or me and my book and my bare feet in the ditch. Yippee! Just then, my mother made a soft noise, and shook her head at my dad. He was on his way downtown, alone. My dad stopped at the soft sound, turned around, looked at me, and smiled.

"Come on, shoes on, let's go do the town!" *Double yippee*!! I thought to myself.

Being on vacation at Grammy's and spending the day with my dad was the best. So, I slipped my feet into my favourite green flip flops and hopped into the front seat of the station wagon. It had no seat belts, but an air conditioner that sat on the hump under the dashboard that would spit ice chips. We backed out of the driveway and onto the dusty road headed to Main Street.

Our first stop would be the Beeline Service Station to visit with my cousin, and what do you know? He had a Snickers candy bar that "somebody must of forgot." So, I took it off his hands.

We hung around the station for a time and then walked across the street so Daddy could see his friend Wally

Gardener at the Bank of Spanish Fork. I wasn't allowed inside the bank because I was a kid, I guess. I don't know for sure if that was a real rule or my Daddy's rule. So, I went up to the corner by the drug store, next to Sonoma's dress shop, took off one green flip flop and dropped it into the ditch.

It was a slow day, so I could just walk beside the ditch down to the next corner and retrieve my shoe, over and over. Today the water was slow. Sometimes the ditch had more water in it and it went really fast. Then I would have had to run along by the gutter and be sure to grab my shoe or it would go down under the road. So today, since the water was so pokey, I decided to see what would happen if my shoe really did go under the road. But the closer my shoe got to the corner, the more I worried. I imagined myself as a poor little eight year old waif with only one green rubber shoe. So at the last minute I grabbed up the shoe, put it on and crossed the street. The ditch still went on, so with both shoes on and a head full of possible adventure, I followed the gutter. It took me past the pipe repair shop where my uncles worked with sheet metal and past the square waffle-looking building.

On the next block there were even more wonderful things to see! Cars—shiny new ones—they smelled wonderful. I wandered all around the cars. Then I passed the grocery store. It was a big one with big letters that didn't spell a real word for a name. It wasn't small like at home and it didn't have a little piggy on the top either, like our store. After the store I saw even more adventure—the fire engine! I hurried past, just in case it needed to go somewhere (by this time, some of my sense of adventure, as well as my feet, were lagging behind).

I was grateful to see the big church with the round steps leading up to the double doors up ahead. That was for sure the neatest church and stairway I'd ever seen! I could go up one side and down the other or mix it up and do it in reverse, which I did. After a short rest, I decided to go just one more block before I turned around and went back. There were people at the first house on the corner. Mrs. Williams was very nice to me when she asked me where I "belonged." She told me that she owned the dress store right at the very beginning of my adventure on the corner by the first drug store. Then she said that the house next to hers belonged to a man that could fix bicycles.

"Mr. Olson hasn't lived there very long," she said. "Only two years." I was amazed—two years was forever in my book. Why, two years ago I was a baby just starting school!

I made a mental note to ask my grandma when I got home if Mr. Olsen was an "Olsen, or an Olson." She would know. She knew everyone's family name by where they lived. The next house had a great front porch with little pink rosebushes all around. I bet that porch was a great place to watch the parade! Except even though it had a big front porch, it didn't look like it had a basement to keep everything from pickles to grandkids cool. I imagined that if a big strong wind came, that pretty house would just go down easy.

The last house on the last street of my travels had a huge side yard. It looked like the perfect house in the flannel board stories from the children's *Friend* magazine! There were no weeds, no flowers, and no yard toys. I wasn't sure if there were real people that lived there or if, like in my imagination, they were perfectly poised, perfectly dressed, smiling people inside. Hmmm.

Just then, I saw my Dad's car pull up and stop on the corner. I carefully watched his face to see if he had any red splotches on his neck. That would mean he was upset at me. No splotches and he was laughing! Whew. He told me to jump into the car and he would take me to Charlie's grill for a hamburger so I could watch Charlie swat a mouse off the grill before he put the burger on! Eek! I knew he was kidding. I got the feeling he was sorry that he'd left me out on Main Street alone for so long....sorta.

DID YOU HEAR THE ONE ABOUT...THE LOST SCHOLAR?

It was early in the school year. The hot, depressing, sticky summer heat had finally dissipated and was replaced by the crisp autumn temperatures. It was too cold to go barefoot; socks and shoes were required, though coats were not yet a necessity. The trees were just beginning to shake themselves loose of their brittle leaves, leaving round piles of brown and red against fences and under the shrubs.

On the East Bench, the canyon breeze had been replaced with a periodic bite of chill wind that would send tiny cyclones of homeless leaves into the road and into the ditches no longer full of irrigation water.

On one particular morning, the young mother sent her husband off to work, cleaned up the breakfast dishes, then bathed and dressed her little two-year-old for the day. She set him free from his nursery with his favorite one-eyed teddy bear to play in the living room while she got dressed for the day herself.

The young mother had planned to take her little boy outside for a walk that would end at her husband's office just in time for lunch. She knew and expected that there were millions of things for them to inspect along the way. She and her son had discussed all the wonderful things they might see along the way to Daddy's for lunch!

She hustled out of the room grabbing a sweater for herself, a jacket for her little boy and the diaper bag that was stuffed with all the necessities for a three block, two hour walk only to find the living room quiet and empty. Calling his name she went from room to room in their little house. The house was very quiet. Too quiet. No giggling of a hiding two-year-old. No tell-tale crumbs of a stolen cookie. She began to feel an anxious pit form in her stomach. She called and searched the small back yard, then all around the house. She crouched on all fours and crawled along the hedge that bordered the side of the house, only to find nothing.

The young couple had not lived in the little corner house for very long and didn't know the neighbors. There was one house that had been turned into several rental apartments on one side and the junior high school filled up the remainder of the block. Next to the junior high was the Central School that was for some elementary students. The young mother was not familiar with the school system in the area. It was all new to her. So… she panicked. She called her husband at work and told him that their little boy was missing and had probably been kidnapped. He first tried to calm her down of course, then jumped into his car and started a systematic tour of the area. When his search proved fruitless he returned to his home to comfort his now distraught wife.

In the meantime…in a Social Studies class in the junior high school, the eighth graders were surprised to see a very confident two-year-old, holding a one-eyed teddy bear walk into the room, choose a desk, with the chair attached, climb upon the chair and sit quietly, smiling at the teacher. The teacher calmly asked if anyone knew their "new student," whereupon one boy laughed and said, "I know him. He just lives in the little house on the corner." The teacher said quietly, not wanting to scare the little thing, "Would you then please return this bear and its rightful owner to his mother?"

Minutes later, there was a joyful reunion and a picnic on the front lawn at the little house on the corner.

HAVE YOU SEEN THIS PLACE?

Sometimes, after you have lived in an area for awhile, you stop seeing it. Whether you are new in town or have lived here all your life, most of you have developed your very own routes through and around this lovely city. You travel these same routes physically while mentally checking off your to do list, listening to the latest scores, weather forecast or traffic report. Of course, you are mindful of traffic and destination and your own personal time clock.

But what if you arrived at your destination by taking a different route? Could it make a refreshing enlightenment to your day? Perhaps you would see something that has always been there, but you never noticed it before. Or by chance, if you looked around, you might see that the flags are out, or at half-staff. How often do you notice that the horse on top of Western Unlimited is a different color? How long did it take you to notice that the very old two-story building on Main Street with the boarded-up windows and the very large sign advertising tattoos has been repainted? The boardedup windows are gone, and there is a lovely awning in front. Hopefully you did notice the rebirth of the old post office into a wellness center. That would be pretty hard to miss.

Not all the changes have gone on only on Main Street. That is one reward caused by road construction. Sometimes you might be forced to reroute your usual destination, or go around the block. There are some old homes that are being carefully restored and some vacant lots that have been cleared and filled with beautiful new houses. This is an opportunity for you to get new ideas for your own front yard, or a new color for your front door. Who knows? You might see that table or old chair that is perfect for your son's dorm room at college… free, on the side of the street!

One thing I am afraid some people may have missed is the new extension of Scenic Drive along the edge of the hill, overlooking the river bottoms. I could tell you to begin on the road at the west side of the cemetery and just keep going, but that would take all the fun out of the exploration.

Speaking of cemeteries, when was the last time you visited the Pioneer Cemetery? Let me begin with an explanation. In approximately 1943 The Daughters of the Utah Pioneers (DUP) gathered their family records and realized that many of the first settlers of this area were buried on the edge of the hill overlooking the river bottoms. That sad little piece of scrub grass had been trampled by grazing cattle for years. Any semblance of headstones or markers had been trod over by the wandering cattle. So the women gathered any remaining pieces of the broken headstones and with gentle prodding (I'm sure), they encouraged their men folks to build a proper marker constructed of those treasured pieces they had scrounged, mixed with large rock and fortified with cement. They made one large structure, looking almost like a barbecue grill with a center marker listing only the names of the people their scanty records revealed, and flanked on each side by lower platforms to place flowers or decoration, forming a T. The women constructed a small fence surrounding the area. The DUP was grateful for the assistance of the Sons of the Pioneers who did all the heavy lifting and the actual construction.

As the years went by, the people in town visited the old cemetery as often as possible. Spanish Fork City had provided a new, well cared for cemetery closer to town that was more accessible and some of the families of the people buried in the old cemetery erected new headstones and burial places for their deceased relatives. Still, some of the stalwart DUP members would take their families up to the marker to have a picnic and while there would tell some pioneer stories.

One woman would march her Sunday school class from the Second Ward Church clear up to the Pioneer Cemetery in order to demonstrate the difficult trek of their ancestors.

The Daughters of the Pioneers South Center Company formed a committee years ago to carefully restore the marker that was set in 1943. Included in that project was the arduous task of researching all the available records of the pioneers that were indeed buried at that first burial site on the edge of the hill. The original marker listed approximately thirty-five pioneer names. After months of searching, the researchers were able to ascertain over 100 pioneers who were interred in the field!

The dedicated women of the DUP organization created and sold cookbooks filled with pioneer recipes. They sold cookies and held a craft fair to raise money for this project. Several citizens and many local businesses donated time, materials and cash in assistance. Spanish Fork City enlisted their various departments to assist in the completion of the park. In cooperation with the developer of the adjacent new subdivision, more of that burial site was included in the new Pioneer Cemetery.

In the meantime, the ladies of the DUP had engaged a local sculptor to build a statue fitting for the new historical site. The bronze statue is of a young pioneer couple with their young family clinging close to each other, standing atop the windy hill and overlooking the beautiful river bottoms with its lush fields and towering poplar trees. Each small grave has a marker. There are eight bronze storyboards with short histories of some of the people who are buried there along the sidewalk surrounding the cemetery. It is a quiet, peaceful oasis in our busy, ever-growing town. In fact, now the subdivision is almost filled with beautiful custom homes. You can find the small cemetery at 1900 South and 1530 East.

Here is a taste of some of the journal entries of the people who settled this little town:

> "This story is about the first family who were buried in the Pioneer Cemetery, and the cemetery was first called the Redd Cemetery."

> "In 1853, John H. Redd's sawmill was burned down by the Indians, a $6,000 loss to the community. November 25th, 1853, John and Elizabeth suffered an even greater loss when their fifteen-year-old son, John Holt Redd, was thrown from a horse and killed. His mother, Elizabeth, heartbroken, died three days later on the 28th. All three were buried in the Redd cemetery now referred to as The Pioneer Cemetery."

This story was a journal entry by Abraham Hunsaker, as he was preparing for the burial of his son, George Hunsaker, and his wife's mother, Mary Gardner Sweeten Luckham in the Pioneer Cemetery:

June 12, 1858: George Sweeten Hunsaker departed this life June 12, 1858 in the morning at sunrise…We prepair the grave of his grandmother Luckham and we bury him by hir side as she called him hir boy on hir deathbed… We buryed him east of Palmyry City some 3 miles north of Spanish Fork half mile on top of the hill."

—*Pat Sandage, researcher*

Chapter 4: People of Spanish Fork

It Begins

The records show that the first settlers to come to Spanish Fork didn't really begin in Spanish Fork. The majority of the first settlers were sent by President Brigham Young to homestead Palmyra.

Case in point would be the Boyack family (go to William Boyack history in Family Search. It tells of him starting out in Palmyra and then to a dugout where the city drug was).

President Young assigned several families to settle Palmyra. However, even though Palmyra was wonderful farm ground, and they liked to plant crops and fish in Utah Lake and keep the livestock there, they preferred the ground to the east better suited for safety. Families wanted to stay together in close proximity for safety reasons as well as for socializing.

The new town of Spanish Fork was basically divided "culturally."

The Welsh families built their homes between 400 North and 800 North, then east from the current Main Street to 800 East.

The Danish built their homes west of the current Main Street between 400 North to 800 North, and from Main street west to 300 West approximately.

The Icelanders set up their own little community east of Main Street, to 10th East and from Center Street to 400 South. They even had their own church! Most, but not all of the Icelanders to emigrate to Utah were members of the Church of Jesus Christ of Latter-day Saints. Some of the immigrants held onto their Lutheran faith from home. So, there was a Lutheran church at the top of Center Street at Tenth North, across from where the Diamond Fork Junior High School is located now.

The English chose the west side of Main from Center Street to 300 South. Years later this area was known as the "Silk Stocking Ward."

In early Spanish Fork there were four wards. It just became common knowledge that if you were in the

Second Ward, for instance, you were probably English. It only makes sense that if you were with family and had left your home in Europe and traveled for months together and liked the same food and spoke the same language, you would naturally settle down comfortably together. Of course there were some interlopers who braved a different neighborhood. Some settled in various areas for the challenge and some due to lack of information. The people who lived outside of these areas were called "new people."

The reason I refer to "Main Street" as "the current Main Street" is because 300 East was at one time supposed to be the Main Street. Have you noticed what a beautiful, wide street this is? It was even once called "Broadway."

Icelandic Monument

LITTLE HISTORY BACKGROUND

When Brigham Young began colonizing the young territory of Utah, he sent some of the early settlers out of Salt Lake farther south to colonize what we now consider "the better part of the state." Some were advised to begin a settlement in what is now Utah County. The area chosen was south and west of Provo, by the lake. President Young called it Palmyra. They built a fort there and began to build shelters and farm the surrounding acres. Several very strong families began to settle that area. One such family began in Maryland. Samuel Simons married Elizabeth Scott. Samuel was later killed in a runaway carriage accident leaving his young wife with four sons, the youngest of which was born a few months after his death. She remarried and moved to Carthage with three of her boys. They decided to travel up the Mississippi river hoping to eventually travel to California. But they liked the rich soil in Illinois and stayed there.

One of Elizabeth Scott's sons, Levan (or Leven), joined the Mormons and he and his family were persecuted and had their crops burned. This son, Leven, moved with the Mormons to Nauvoo. They had planned to leave Nauvoo with one of the first groups but someone needed his team, so Leven gave it to him, sold his remaining $1,500 farm for $250 and bought another team and left Nauvoo with the next group.

Leven and his family would travel with a group, stop and plant crops, repair wagons, make tubs and barrels only to leave again still heading west. On one part of his travels they came upon the swollen Sweetwater River. They had to choose to either wait three weeks there for the water to subside, or head north into country filled with buffalo and Indians. The buffalo were an excellent supply of meat and hides, but the Indians were frightening and antagonistic. Leven and his camp chose to head north.

Going this direction, they met up with some friendly Indians who would sell them fresh elk as well as some threatening warriors who were fighting other tribes. It took great courage to move peacefully between the warring Snake and Shoshone Indian tribes.

They finally arrived in Salt Lake City but stayed only for a short time to rest. Then they were advised to move south to Springville. Once in Springville, they built a small cabin only to have the Indians kill all their pigs and chickens.

It was thanks to Stephen Markham from Spanish Fork that they finally set up a real homestead west of Spanish Fork on Markham's north quarter section on the banks of the Spanish Fork River.

The Simmons family is an example of the sturdiness and courage that is the core of the people who settled in Spanish Fork. Their family has grown and prospered and now have generations who call Lakeshore their home.

Wait!—Leven Simmons started in Maryland, traveled to Nauvoo, moved across the west headed for California only to finally stop in Salt Lake. Before he could even get settled, Brigham Young sent him south to Palmyra. Leven was a trustee of the first school district in Spanish Fork as well as the Mayor in 1863. Recently, (in historic terms) his family merged with the Gordon family and are one of the stronghold families of Lakeshore.

JOHN MOORE 1838-1920
Excerpts from the "Biography of John Moore" by Leora Hughes Andrus

John Moore was born October 4, 1838 in a small village in Darbyshire, England. When he was only two years old his mother died and he was taken care of by his grandmother. When he was six years old his father died, leaving him and his brother Joseph, who was four years his senior, orphans. The maternal grandparents took the responsibility for caring for the boys.

About the year 1846, one Henry George, an elder of the Church of Jesus Christ of Latter-day Saints, obtained work of the grandparents' family, and much to the astonishment of the neighborhood, converted and baptized six of the seven brothers, also the father and mother.

In December 1850, two uncles, John and David West, with their families and a second cousin, Alfred Longman and his family, made preparations to come to America. David West, with the consent of Johns' grandmother and by the advice of the president of Derbyshire Conference, took John into his family and brought him to America. His grandfather, William West died two years previous to this.

The ship, Martha Ellen, was chartered January 8, 1851. They set sail for America. Captain John T. Davis was in charge of this ship to New Orleans. Captain Davis and John Moore were life-long friends. They arrived in New Orleans march 14, 1851. The family he was with went to St. Joseph, Missouri, arriving there April 23, 1851. While there, John worked at a brickyard for three months, also as a helper in a hotel and then for ten months in a clothing store where he gained some knowledge of business.

May 20, 1853, his uncle, David West and his family started for Salt Lake City, taking John, who was how in his fifteenth year, with them. They arrived in Salt Lake City, September 27, 1853. John had to make his own living, so he worked May 20, 1853, his uncle, David West and his family started for Salt Lake City, taking John, who was how in his fifteenth year, with them.

They arrived in Salt Lake City, September 27, 1853. John haat various jobs wherever he was fortunate enough to get employment. In 1835 his brother Joseph and his wife arrived in Salt Lake City.

In the spring of 1856 provisions in Salt Lake City were very scarce. John had trouble finding work, so at the suggestion of his uncle, Jesse West, John traveled south on foot and arrived in Provo where he was able to obtain work. He remained in Provo until September of that same year. Then he moved farther south to Spanish Fork. He labored in various capacities until 1860.

On October 1, 1860, he was married by Bishop Stephen Markham to Caroline Hicks who was born March 1, 1844, in Nauvoo, Illinois. Unfortunately, she died May 9, 1878. To John and Caroline Hicks Moore were born eight children, three sons and five daughters, and a nephew, John T. Moore, who was left an orphan at the age of four and was raised as a member of the John Moore family.

In the early sixties, John Moore was elected captain of the company of infantry of the Nauvoo Legion, and afterward was promoted to major in the legion and held that office until its disbandment by Black, then acting governor of Utah Territory.

John Moore was a public man. He held public offices for thirty-five years, acting as alderman, city councilman, and recorder. The last office named he held for thirteen years. He met with the State Legislature in 1894. He served as county judge for six years. He assisted in the organization of the Spanish Fork Cooperative Institution in 1894. He was connected with the institution for over twenty-five years, acting in the capacity of salesman, superintendent, secretary, treasurer and bookkeeper.

John Moore took a keen interest in education. He served as school trustee for several terms. He might be termed a self educated man. He was well-read in most topics, and well versed in literature. He was inclined to be poetical as well as musical. He was a supporter of the old Spanish Fork band. He was a member of the old Spanish Fork choir and for years a active member of the Spanish Fork Third Ward choir. He was a faithful Sunday school worker and for many years a home missionary. He watched with interest the construction of the Third Ward Chapel and just the day before his last sickness began, he walked down to see how the work was progressing. He was very charitable and generous to those in need. He believed firmly in not letting the left hand know what the right hand was doing in this respect, thus many of his good deeds were never known. He had the love, respect, and confidence of his many friends, both young and old.

February 11, 1920 he suffered a stroke and died as a result on February 22, 1920, at his home in Spanish Fork. From the time of his marriage until that of his death, he knew no other home. All his children were born there and both he and his wife died there. He was a widower for 44 years, keeping his family together until they were all married.

This is an example of the kind of legacy there is in Spanish Fork. Just imagine, a young orphan leaving what little family he had left and coming to America. Then working at any job he could find to earn his passage to Salt Lake. He was a self-educated, unemployed immigrant who walked to Provo to seek employment, and ended up as a husband, father of eight, a legislator, judge, and city councilman to name a few titles he held. Some of his family still lives in Spanish Fork.

ALBERT SWENSON 1872-1968-

Albert Swenson was born December 16, 1872 in Spanish Fork, Utah to August Swenson and Bertha Olsen Persson. His family owned land, cattle and sheep. They used the wool form the sheep to make all of their own clothing.

The first school in Spanish Fork was an adobe building across the road west from his father's home. It is where the old Reese school stands. Albert was a good reader and also good in arithmetic. He was called the "walking primer" because he memorized the whole book. He had a very good memory. He attended school during the winter months, after plowing was done.

Albert met Sina Diantha Nielson at a dance in Rastus Nelson's new home. Dances were held in the new homes before the families moved in. Albert danced three or four times with Sina that night and it was the beginning of a great courtship and marriage. Albert married Sina Diantha Nielsen on February 9, 1898 in the Manti LDS temple.

Their first home was rented from Butlers on Eighth East and First North, for $30 a year. They lived there one year, and then moved to a larger home of Mortensen's, then into Dudley's for $42 a year.

He purchased a lot for $225, where his present home now stands, on the northwest corner of the block where the old 4th Ward church stood and where the current new 10th Ward church stands.

Albert was called on a Swedish mission after he was married. He studied the Swedish language. Though it was very difficult, he and his companion were involved with the conversion of three members, two of which were an older couple who wanted to join the Mormon Church.

Albert's wife, Sina, lived alone and his father August managed Albert's farm and interests while he was on his mission in Sweden for 2 ½ years. Albert owed his Father $29 before he left. August said to Albert, "If you accept this mission call and fulfill it honorably, you will be out of debt when you return home."

When Albert returned home from Sweden he borrowed $700 from his Father to build his new home on 490 North 300 East in Spanish Fork. He hauled sand from the lake and bought and hauled the new brick.

Albert and Sina had five children. Harold, Rulon, Norma, Leah and Allen. Rulon and Rhea were married in December 1922 and moved in with the whole Albert Swenson family. Allen passed away in October 1928 and Sina passed away, at age 54, in January 1930. Harold, Norma, and Leah were married a few years later and moved out of the home. Rulon and Rhea lived with and took care of Albert for 45 ½ years.

Albert was a kind, understanding, and appreciative person, and very helpful in the home and yard. He went to the farm with the men until he was in his nineties. Albert had good health and a strong body, and an exceptionally bright, mind. He spoke in hundreds of funerals, and quoted poetry fluently, which was such a comfort to the mourners and congregations.

He was a very religious man in every respect. He read and memorized the scriptures daily. He read beneath a light bulb, hanging from an electric cord in the middle of the kitchen celling.

Albert passed away Saturday, May 25, 1968 from an injury he had sustained when he fell off his front porch on Monday, May 20, 1968. He died in the Payson Hospital and was buried in the Spanish Fork Cemetery.

HAROLD ALBERT SWENSON
Farming history as told by himself on March 13, 1974

I was born at our home (southeast corner of 300 East 500 South) in Spanish Fork on February 3, 1899. I am the eldest of five—two brothers, Rulon and Allen, and two sisters, Norma and Leah.

I remember as a young boy hoeing and topping and thinning sugar beets. We would haul the beets to the Leland Sugar Factory, a few miles from Spanish Fork. One of the highlights of our trip was waiting for Dad (Albert Swenson) to bring us burnt sugar out of the factory to eat.

We would haul hay on a flat-bed wagon pulled by horses. When the hay was cut we would make small piles of hay up and down the rows. A day or two before we would haul it we had to turn the piles over with a pitch fork so they could dry. We would haul the hay by one or more of us standing on the wagon and tromping the hay down as it was forked up.

We had to feed and milk the cows every night and morning. We separated the cream so we could make our butter, cottage cheese and have our own buttermilk. Another responsibility I had was to bring in the coal and wood for the coal stove.

When I think back on how we used to farm, I think of our means of transportation to and from the farm, the team and wagon. I recall very vividly getting up in the middle of the night, taking the lantern and getting on the old gray mare to go to the river bottoms to irrigate. Farming now is easy in comparison to what it was. In the past few years I have leveled one hundred and some odd acres of ground. Along with that, we have installed cement ditches whereby it is a pleasure now to irrigate.

When I think about the accidents I've been through in my life, I feel like I have a mission to fulfill. I recall coming home from the ranch one cold, wintery morning with the tractor and the spreader. I heard three sharp whistles and the next thing I knew the spreader was down the train track and demolished. I sat on the tractor within a foot of the track. At that time I was bishop of the ward and I often told them I had better quit. But after that accident I felt the Lord had spared my life and I really did have a mission to fulfill.

I remember the privilege of working as a young boy side by side with my father for over fifty years. I have valued what he taught me and tried to impart some of my learning to my son. I take great pride in my son Ray Allen's accomplishment of winning for three straight years the most yield of a corn crop in the state of Utah.

I feel my life as a farmer has been one of hard work and struggle. But the benefits I've received from such a life, far outweigh any other way of life I might have chosen. I feel satisfied that I have made my place in the world on my own, through diligence and hard work. Having lived a large portion of my life and looking back, I would have lived my life the same way again.

JENNIE ALBERTA WILLIAMS SWENSON
As told by Loa Swenson Schwartz and Donna Swenson Burt

Jennie Alberta Williams Swenson: born July 16, 1900 in Spanish Fork, Utah. She was born in the family home. Her parents were David William and Sarah (Sadie) Evans Williams.

Jennie attended school until the age of 16. At that time someone for First Security Bank that knew the family came to the house and asked David if he had any daughters that would like to come and work at the bank. All of her older sisters said no but Jennie said she would like to work at the bank. They were sure she was too young but she convinced them to give her a try. She dropped out of school in about the 8th grade in order to do this. She did very well at the job and dearly loved the work. She worked form age 16 to age 26 when she had her first child, Loa.

They had very little clothes in those days so she would come home form work and wash out her work clothes by hand so she could wear them the next day.

Grandma worked at the bank during the great depression. The employees knew that the bank was going to close but were not allowed to tell anyone. Jennie tried to suggest to her dad that he should draw some of his money out. He told her he would take care of his own business and for her not to worry. The bank did close and the whole town lost their savings. This was very hard on her.

Jennie married Harold Albert Swenson on February 20, 1923 in the Salt Lake Temple by Joseph F. Smith or Joseph Fielding Smith. Their first child, Loa Jean was born three years later on November 21, 1926. Ray Allen was born February 12, 1930. Wallace Harold was born on December 19, 1932 and died at 16 months old of a mastoid ear infection in April of 1933. Donna was born February 4, 1934, and their last child was Phyllis who was born April 2, 1939.

When they were first married they lived a few months with Harold's parents, Albert and Alsina (Sina) Diantha Nielsen Swenson. They then bought a house on 400

North between 400 and 500 East on the north side of the road. A brown duplex is now in its place.

When the children lived in the house on 400 North, they caught most of the childhood diseases. In those days they would put a big QUARINTENE sing on the wall by the front door. No one was allowed in the house. Loa and Ray Allen got scarlet fever and were extremely ill. Loa also got rheumatic fever in the same year. It was in this house that Wallace got a mastoid ear infection and died. Donna got the measles as well. In those days the doctors and nurses would come to the home to treat the sick and deliver babies.

When the children were younger, Jennie had to heat all of the wash water on a coal burning stove in a double boiler. She would put the whites in the double boiler on the stove and stir them with a big wooden stick while they boiled. She used homemade lye soap for her washing and bluing for the whites. She would transfer the clothes with a big wooden stick to the washer and then ring them out and put them into a rinse tub. She would rinse and ring them out again and then hang them outside on the line to dry. In the winter the clothes would freeze to the clothes lines. Washing was an all day process.

She always bottled her own fruits (peaches, pears, apricots, cherries, and grapes) as well as pickles of all kinds, red beets, tomatoes and jams. When the girls

(Loa, Donna and Phyllis) came home from school they would help with the peeling and bottling. Jennie would always insist on placing the fruit in the bottles herself so each piece faced out. She loved showing her friends and neighbors all the bottled fruit and took great pride in how they looked.

In the Spanish Fork July 24th parade, Jen would ride on a float, with Sye Snell, honoring the Black Hawk Indians (the Indians native to this area). She had striking dark skin and hair so she would always be chosen to dress as the female Indian. She had a beautiful white leather fringed and beaded dress with moccasins and a feather head band to match.

In 1938 or 1939 when Jennie was pregnant with Phyllis, they moved to her parent's home on 1400 East 800 North to take care of Jen's father David. Phyllis was born in the Hughes Hospital in Spanish Fork shortly after the move. She was their only child born in a hospital. She took are of her father for about five years.

Jen was a very compassionate person. She was always taking food to the sick or needy and sang at almost all the funerals. She and Harold took food baskets to the widows and visited the sick regularly.

As Jen cooked and cleaned she would always whistle—she wouldn't even realize she was doing it. She was a home body and loved working and cleaning around her house. She could always find something to do. She made all her children and grandchildren quilts. Some of the grandchildren's favourite memories are of playing under the quilts as they were in the frames being quilted. Grandpa loved having all the family together on these occasions. One of our favorite meals while having a quilting get-together was cold tomatoes (bottled by Jen), corn fritters and corned beef. Jen was always willing to fix this for all of us whenever we requested it.

Melba King—Memories Of Growing Up

My memories of Spanish Fork go back at least eighty-five years and most of all my memories in this city are good. I am so thankful everyday that my ancestors left their homes and settled in Spanish Fork. The city has changed and grown since I was a little girl and lived on Sixth East and First South in my grandpa Henry Gardner's home. When he and my grandma Elizabeth Martell Gardner were married they already had their home to move into. I often wonder how my grandma provided for herself and two children while Grandpa served a mission for the LDS Church in Oklahoma. Grandma died when she was fifty-seven from complications from a fall out of the granary and broke her hip, and at that time the doctors did not know how to take care of a broken hip. She also developed diabetes which eventually caused her death.

When Grandpa Gardner was seventy years old he had a stroke, which affected his speech and walking. He needed help. So, father and mother, Raymond and Lenore Gardner Gull moved in and helped him for eight years. We had a large windmill outside our kitchen door and if the wind didn't blow, we did not have drinking water. My folks, Ray and Lenore Gull and our family of five girls—Beatrice, Donna, Melba, Elizabeth and Lila—had a half block to enjoy. We had a garden, an orchard, a pasture for the cows, some chickens, and a large grape arbor. It was a wonderful place to grow up in.

Grandpa died at the age of seventy-eight. Our family lived one more year there and then moved to 27 North 200 West in Spanish Fork. I remember the old neighborhood. It was the best! Uncle Dave Lewis lived across the street east. Aunt Annie Holt and her daughter, Mattie lived in the house across the street to the north. Bill and Helga Johnson lived a block to the east of Uncle Dave Lewis. The Halversons lived south of Uncle Dave and the Benjamin and Serald Riches family lived on the corner. Across the street was Mary Higginson, who later became the city librarian. East of Mary was the Sarah Warner family—Dona, Jarvis, Fern, Blair, Eunice, Allen and Reed. Lew and Alta Holt lived on the west corner and the Bill and Eleanor Jarvis family lived on the southwest corner.

George Jex and his wife Della and their children Bill, Melvin, Sterling, Donna and Ronald lived catty-corner to Lew Holt. There were only four houses to most blocks at that time.

Now, if you check, the blocks are filled with houses. It is more difficult to get acquainted with our neighbors because of television, Internet, etc.

We loved all the neighbors and at that time we thought we knew everyone in town. Tim-boy Bearnson would sell us fresh milk for only five cents, the Wilford Johnson family, the Earl Warner family and the Clegg family were all wonderful people. To the north of us lived the Harold Simons family, then Victor and Mary Leifson and across the street was Bishop Arthur McKell and Mark McKell is still living and is 96 years old! Clarence and Lola Johnson Argyle lived east of Bishop McKell and his family, and between them lived the Bill and Mabel Warner family. Then, on the corner was the Hales family. West of Clarence Argyle was the Evans, B. Davis and Daisy, then the Jenkins family—Boyd, Donna and the children.

This was a wonderful place to grow up. At that time the city ended on Eighth East. The Gil Bearnson family lived by where the Icelandic monument is now. They had one son named Sherman and twelve girls. Also, Paul and Hanna Valgardson lived with them. At that time the population was about 5,000 and is now about 39,000 and still growing!

One day when I was about nine years old out by the lilac bush I had the hose running when the city Water Master saw me and scared me to death! Bill Lloyd was the

Water Master and we must have been short of culinary water and did he give me the devil for having the water running in the daytime! Needless to say, today we have better water supply, but the demand is so much greater with automatic washers, sprinkler systems and so much greater demands for water. I wonder if we need another mean Water Master?

Our city has had good mayors and city councilmen and we are now a growth state. Congratulations to all the good citizens who have served and those who are serving at this time to make Spanish Fork a great city to live in.

RUTH LEIFSON-
Ruth Leifson is one of the "stalwart Spanish Fork people" I spoke of in the introduction. She has all the criterion of a "stalwart." She was born Ruth Nelson and lived on the west side of Main on 800 North. That puts her in the Danish part of town with all the other Nelsons.

She was raised during the depression and World War II. Her mother had four boys and only one daughter. The boys helped the father with the farming duties outside while Ruth helped her mother with all the cooking, cleaning and sewing.

The following are taken from pages of her personal notebook in her own beautiful cursive handwriting discussing her experiences as a growing girl in Spanish

Fork from the nineteen hundreds right into 2015. These are her memories. What we need to remember is that many people have similar experiences of the exact time, place and event. They are not remembered by everyone in the same way.

Luckily, there are many people living in town today that are close to Ruth's age. They also have had similar experiences. (They remember where they could get a five cent ice cream cone!) Unfortunately, many of us are so proud of the accomplishments of our generation that we give little credence to the past generation's example. In Ruth's childhood they made their own soap, bottled the vegetables they grew themselves, sewed their own clothes and really were forced by the culture to follow the later counsel of President Spencer W. Kimball, "Use it up, wear it out, or do without." And they did without much of the time. But they didn't feel persecuted. They were proud of their productivity and the way they solved given problems.

In Ruth's day, if a person wanted to share a message with a friend, that person would walk over to the friend's house and share the information.

In Ruth's day, if you needed farming equipment or fabric for a new dress, you could go down on Main Street and buy it. Sometimes, if you really needed that certain item downtown and you were short on money, you could maybe make a deal with the proprietor to trade services for goods.

Many times, the younger generations believe that whatever is newer, quicker, or bigger is better.

"Not so," says Ruth's generation. To them, generally speaking, face time or time spent together to complete a project with exactness wins. Her generation prefers the beauty of a creation to the swiftness of completion.

CHILD'S BAKERY—EVA AND HENRY CHILDS
By Nina Childs

Eva told me about going to the Salt Lake Temple to get married. The entire wedding party went by horse and buggy, with a stop overnight at the hotel in Lehi, making the trip an event of several days. What a change to now! Many people drive an hour to a Salt Lake event and to home after on the same evening.

Eva told me about going to the Salt Lake Temple to get married. The entire wedding party went by horse and buggy, with a stop overnight at the hotel in Lehi, making the trip an event of several days. What a change to now! Many people drive an hour to a Salt Lake event and to home after on the same evening.

Henry's oldest son, Lynn, liked to tell the story of how Henry handled a problem: Lynn and his teenage friends made and bottled beer in the basement of the bakery using supplies from the store like yeast and sugar. Henry discovered it and told Lynn to not do that again. Later when Henry caught the teens with a large amount ready to bottle, he didn't say a word but went upstairs and got a very large scoop full of salt and returned to the boys in the basement and silently poured all the salt in their drink. The surprised boys continued and bottled the drink, but it had so much salt they could never drink it. This ended their escapades of bottling beer in the bakery in the basement.

Child's bakery business in 1957 when I was still working at Geneva as a secretary, but I soon became involved with the bakery. We then added a wedding catering business, Nina's Catering, where we furnished food, wedding cake, decorations and everything for a wedding reception. We did this until Cleve died in 1992. Two weeks later my daughter, Diana and I added the Dancewear business, but kept the Health Food Supplement part of the Bakery's Health Food Business, expanding it. Also, I continued teaching dance for a few more years which I had done previously for many years with my sister and daughter.

Today my daughter Diana Child Nixon and I are actively engaged in the business of "Child's Health and Dancewear" at 125 North Main in Spanish Fork. I consider it an opportunity and a blessing to have work in our business every day but Sunday, and I believe it is a great part of the good health I enjoy at my advanced age. It is almost 2015 and I have no plans to retire from our business.

THE MARDON CAFE—1946-1949-
by Don and Carolyn Robertson

George Victor Robertson became the manager of the Spanish Fork J. C. Penney store in about 1940. The store was located where the Stone Drug is at present. He was personable, honest, efficient, and well liked. About 1946 the managers in Payson, Spanish Fork and Springville were all forced to quit. They were men who had helped build up the company over the years. Having no bitterness, Victor looked forward to owning his own business.

An opportunity soon came; two brothers, Ed and Harry Elmer had a confectionery and café business two doors south of the J. C. Penney Store which they were anxious to sell, and the Robertsons bought the business.

When sons, Mark and Don arrived home from the navy, a major remodeling was underway. Victor hired his sons and a number of their friends to help. They erected a wall across the back which made space for a full size modern kitchen. Equipment was purchased and installed for a soda fountain with stools. Booths were installed with new red simulated-leather benches.

The staff was hired. Harry Elmer, famous for his hand-dipped chocolates, stayed on as candy maker. He dipped the chocolates in a shop in the basement where the temperature was ideal for them to cure. They would be stored on racks, and were often "tested" by the family employees as they passed by. Juanita Guild was hired to help with the fountain because of her experience. Many foods were still rationed because of the war, but Mark was able to buy extra sugar with his veteran status which helped to get the fountain going.

An ice cream machine and a large freezer to cure and store it in were soon purchased. They learned to freeze delicious ice cream with a large variety of flavor including some unusual ones for the time—green pineapple, orange coconut, and root beer. All of the ice cream was hand dipped earlier into cartons, milk shakes, malts or cones.

The grand opening finally came of The Mardon Café and Confectionery, named after sons Mark and Don. Money was still quite tight following the war, but townspeople came to congratulate and offer their support.

As manager, Vic spent long hours at the café, often twelve hours a day. He soon mastered all of the skills necessary including a major skill of loving and caring for people. Years later, people often told the family of something he did or said which influenced them for good. He was an optimist and encouraged others to be thankful and appreciative of what they had. He insisted on quick service and customer satisfaction and invited comments as patrons left.

The entire family was involved in the new enterprise. His wife, Lucile, became famous for the homemade cakes she baked for the café. Customers would ask, "Are any of Lucille's cakes left?" Their daughter Sheronne became a skillful waitress and fountain operator. Mark arrived early in the morning to open the café and make the ice cream. He also basked the pies and prepare the roast beef and roast pork for the day. Sheronne and Don peeled potatoes, washed dishes, waited tables, and often closed up at night. Everything was served in glass or china so there were always plenty of dishes to wash.

A hot "merchant's luncheon" was offered at noon. The main staples on the menu were hot beef or hot pork sandwiches, which included potatoes, gravy and vegetables, all for 85 cents. The café was open from 5:00 a.m. to 1:00 a.m.

Eventually there was a full staff of employees—Juanita Guild, Ivie L, Laura Shepherd, Pearl Davis, Beulah Monk, Elaine Jones, Cliff Huff, Bernice, and others. The waitresses wore uniforms which were white dresses with red and blue trim and white caps.

The biggest day of the year was the 24th of July. Spanish Fork celebrated with a parade, carnival, and rodeo, attracting people from all over the county. Hamburger patties were pre-made, French fries pre-cut, and ice cream stored for the big day. Everyone worked long hours, with Vic working 18 hours, however he was never seen sad or grumpy. By 1:00 a.m. the café was empty of food, and every dish dirty, but after a second wind, the whole crew would get to work and the café would soon be ready for another day.

Vic purchased a soft ice cream machine which was very unique. The price was five cents for a small cup and ten cents for a large. The shakes at the fountain were made with hand-dipped ice cream, milk, flavored syrup, and mixed in an electric malt machine. They were a delicious treat, but they were very time consuming for the waiters and waitresses. After a school dance, the cafe would fill every booth with students. Almost everyone ordered a hamburger a malt or milk shake. It required a lot of effort to hand dip the hard ice cream until all orders were filled.

After the store closed at night Sheronne and Don sometimes put a nickel in the jukebox and danced and sang while cleaning the fountain and mopping the floor. After the sons left on their missions, Sherrone would sometimes close the café alone. Willard Vincent, the local policeman escorted her home in his police car for protection.

In 1947, Mark and Don were called to serve missions in Denmark, so Vic had an extra work load. Other challenges faced the family; new fast food places were opening in town and nearby. The Angelus movie theater (now Boothe Music) burned to the ground. Theater patrons would often come for popcorn and treats to take to the movie, as they were not sold in theaters at the time. Many would come in after the movie to purchase ice cream to take home. With two sons on missions, Sheronne attending BYU, and income drastically reduced, it was a struggle to be able to send the required money to the missionaries each month. But in answer to prayer, Vic was assured they would be taken care of, and the burden was lifted.

Victor had an opportunity to go into a partnership with pharmacist Horace Magleby, so they chose to close the Mardon Café and open Magleby Drug in the same location, ending a great chapter in the Robertson family and on Main Street.

GLADES DRIVE-IN

By Sharlene Schwartz Irvine

Glade's Drive-In has long been an institution in Spanish Fork. It even featured on the cover of a BYU magazine at one time. It also has its own Facebook page with many followers. It was one of the two original fast food restaurants in town.

Glade and Loa Schwartz were the original founders and owners of Glade's Drive-In. They bought it about 1957 when it was an Arctic Circle. Later the name was changed to Glade's Drive-In. Glade and Loa owned and operated it for 20 years. Glade's was the originator of the "famous white sauce" for French fries. In addition to their white sauce, Glade's was known far and wide for their fish and chips. There were several families from out of state that always stopped for an order of fish and chips every time they traveled through the state. Many people still believe they make the best hamburgers and shakes around. Their French fries were peeled and sliced daily (about 500 pounds of potatoes). They also sold penny candy. Each piece cost one cent. They would place your candy in a white hamburger bag and it didn't take long to fill the bag at one cent a piece.

When Glade's Drive-In began, these are the prices they charged for the various food items:

Hamburger...$0.25
Fries...$0.10
Drinks..$0.10
Malts..$0.25
Fish and chips..................................$0.79
Shrimp and chips.............................$0.89

Most days Glade's fed lunch and after school snack items to most of the high school students in Spanish Fork since the school was just across the street to the south (Nebo School District offices are there now).

It was also a custom for many of the little league coaches to treat their teams to ice creams or malts if they won their baseball games.

Throughout the years Glade's has provided jobs for many of the high school girls in town. Some even continued working for as long as thirty years.

In 1977 Glade and Loa Schwartz sold Glade's Drive-In to Brent Johnston. Brent retained the name of Glade's Drive-In but he has owned and operated the drive-in since then.

SMALL-TOWN EATERY A STAPLE—AND A LEGEND

by Rodger L. Hardy, Deseret News staff writer; July 4, 2000

SPANISH FORK—It was a sweltering summer day when Tom Reece left his Orem home on a mission: to wet his whistle with a milk shake from Glade's Drive-In.

Reece has made the 30-mile round trip to the popular Spanish Fork burger joint and shake place for more than 25 years, sometimes as often as every week.

"The food's good, and the cheeseburgers are great," he said of the place that some folks say makes the best shakes in Utah Valley.

On that hot day last week, he ordered only a strawberry shake. But when he gets a hankering for a burger, Glade's, which has become a legendary landmark along tree-lined Main Street, is the place to go for hot-off-the-grill goods.

Owner Brent Johnston buys meat from local cattlemen several times a week. He boasts that not an ounce of the meat cooked at his establishment has ever been frozen.

Jill Olsen, who frequented the red-and-white painted drive-in when she was a student at Spanish Fork High School in the 1970s, now lives in Hurricane. But when she pops into town, Glade's is on her menu.
"We went there a lot," she recalled from her high school days. "For $1.25 you could get a hamburger, fries and a drink."

She also remembers the bags of penny candy. "You didn't need a whole lot of money to get a lot of candy," she said.

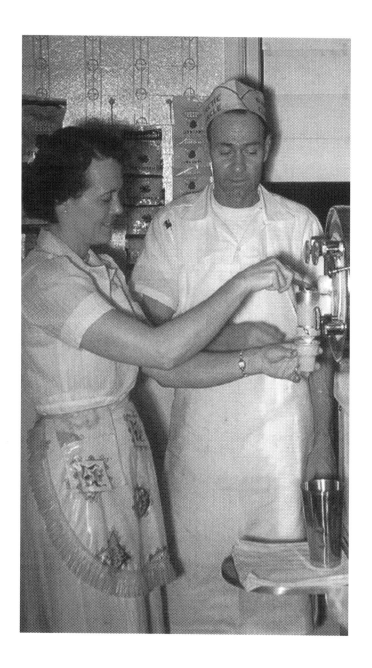

Glade's was even a topic in her high school business class, Olsen said. Her teacher used it as an example of how a person could purchase a business; hold it for a decade, then sell at a profit.

Once an Arctic Circle, Glade Schwartz didn't want to turn the place into a sit-down restaurant as the food chain wanted back in 1962, he said. So, he changed the signage to bear his name. It was across the street from what was then a junior high school.

"I had no desire to have all those kids inside," he said. "We didn't have the room or the parking."

"Glade used to be the chief of police," Johnston said. "I got to know him from him being chief of police and me being a teenager."

That, too, was back in the 1960s when police chiefs in small towns kept a watchful eye on the local teens.

"It was just, 'Keep your nose clean and I'll give you a ride home,'" Johnston said. Then, he'd receive an invitation to work on Schwartz's farm. Now 73, Schwartz still operates his farm.

Later, Johnston had a son who needed medical care from Primary Children's Hospital in Salt Lake City that his insurance wouldn't cover.

To pay the medical bills, he went to work during evenings at Glade's, where his wife was then working. With the intent of eventually buying the eatery, Johnston persuaded Schwartz to teach him the business. That was 23 years ago.

Many of today's employees are the children of the shop's first workers. Some things have changed, but much of the business remains the same, he said.

Workers at the counter still memorize the orders, rather than write them down, and shakes are still made from scratch. "That was the way I was taught to do it," he said.

Glade's reputation has spread. One day a group from Canada dropped by for some ice cream. They drove 50 miles out of their way to stop at Glade's, Johnston said.

Others stop by for the white sauce that's served with fries.

"It's kinda famous," Johnston said modestly.

While Denise Bennett has worked at Glade's 21 years, only one other person has been at the drive-in longer than Johnston.

Come September, Janet Hansen will have worked there 24 years. She started while she was in high school.

"That's kind of a record for the fast-food business," Johnston mused.

Both she and her husband worked at Glade's for seven years before he found another job.

Hansen usually works nights so she can care for her children during the day.

"He's good to work around my schedule," she said. "He takes good care of me."

GLADE'S COMMUNITY CONNECTION
by Kacie Johnson, Spanish Fork Press; November 15, 2006

Keeping Your Business in Spanish Fork

The scent of down home cooking can linger at any given moment if you're near Glade's Drive-In in Spanish Fork. This one-of-a-kind burger refuge has been luring customers of all ages in since 1954. So how do they stay so successful? One taste of a 'Super Cheese' or strawberry shake will answer that for you. "You'll never work harder for anyone else than you will for yourself," says owner Brent Johnston, who has been at it for thirty years.

Much of Glade's menu is made from scratch such as fish and chips, onion rings and sherbets. "I took the recipes from the previous owner, but the sherbet is my own," said Johnston. While on the subject, I had to ask about the coveted 'white sauce'. Johnston's only response—"It has mayo and stuff." He also took the secret recipe from previous owner Glade Schwartz, and is not about to reveal the ingredients anytime soon. Just to give an idea of its popularity, Johnston says he goes through about 360 pounds each year.

Quality customer service and employee training are a must at Glade's. Denise Bennet and Janet Hansen have been by Johnston's side for almost as long as he's been there. Employees are trained on providing outstanding customer service and product knowledge. "Orders aren't written, but shouted to the cook who must remember a lot at one time. They are really good at it though," Johnston says.

Glade's Drive-In is located at the corner of 300 South and Main. New winter hours are from 10 a.m. to 10 p.m. Monday through Thursday, 10 a.m. to 11 p.m. Friday and Saturday and 11 a.m. to 10 p.m. Sundays.

This story appeared in Spanish Fork Press on page A6.

LYNN JONES

Now here is a man who was born and raised in Spanish Fork. He is well known by many people for many different reasons. In this town, he either taught you, taught with you, farmed with you, worked with you, befriended you or was related to you!

In early morning, Lynn, as a young boy would drive cows from his home on the northwest part of town six or seven blocks to the pasture on the other side of the train tracks. Well, really, the horse drove the cows. Lynn was just riding the horse! His job was to outguess the train that was coming from the north. He kept those cows moving at just the right speed in the right direction so that they would be across the tracks before the train would come. If they were dawdling, the train would blow its whistle and blast them, and the engineer would shake his fist at the boy and horse for cutting things just a little too close. The train would whoosh by, spewing gravel and dust. Lynn could still hear the whistle as they lumbered the rest of the way to the pasture.

He had a neighbor, Mr. Snyder who had lovely little flowers in his yard, by the side of the road. The Jones' milk cows really liked those pretty little flowers and would meander over there for a nibble as Lynn was driving them to pasture. Mr. Snyder would get so mad! He'd holler out the door, "Watch those cows! Keep them away from my flowers!" Cows don't listen. And try as hard as he could, there was always at least one who would head off toward Snyder's as they passed by. Finally, Mr. Snyder called the police. Mr. Argyle, the city cop, stopped by and surveyed the damage. He pushed his cap back, looked at Mr. Snyder and looked at Lynn and the tail end of his cows going on down the road. He then, softly suggested that Mr. Snyder put up a fence between the flowers and the road which was probably not paved. Problem solved.

Consider the life Lynn lived. When he was young, they lived in town and farmed out of town. His family had about a quarter of the city block with a home, barn, milk cows, pigs, horses, and probably at least one dog. Once each week he and his horse would pull a large wagon to the Neilsen-Rick creamery to get whey for the pigs. He and his dad would haul milk from their cows up to Salt Lake to the creamery. Picture this: the two-lane road at the point of the mountain was such a hard pull that Lynn could walk alongside the truck and pick up cans and chuck them into the side of the truck. As a matter of fact, that's how he improved his baseball pitching arm!

Lynn put in curb and sidewalks all over town. He also worked for Vernon Hurst Construction to put in the water tower on the east side of town. He worked with Bud Swanner, Dale Barney, Bill Nelson and Mel Hudman.

He taught at the old middle school (which was on the corner of 300 East and 100 North), and the Benjamin K-3 school. Unfortunately, that school building is lost to us. It looked like the Thurber School. He either taught or was Principal in Springville, Payson and Salem. When he was Principal of the Salem elementary school, he worked with a first grade teacher named Ann Hanks. She was such an incredible teacher that her students could write in cursive by the end of the school year! He was even "lucky enough" to have been the Principal of the new Spanish Fork Middle School-Junior High. That was when the 6th and 7th grades were on one side of the building and the 8th and 9th grades were on the other with a chain fence dividing the two sides.

One time, the sixth graders had a special visitor, McGruff the big dog who protects children from strangers! McGruff was really Arlo Mitchell in costume. He went to the chain fence at lunchtime when the hallway was filled with students, rattled the chains and growled! The children were terrified and ran to Mr. Jones for protection. Mr. Jones calmed the children down, showed McGruff and his handler the door and made note of the event, suggesting the chain fence be removed. The classrooms were open concept so you could hear what teachers were saying in the different classrooms. That concept didn't last very long.

This man farmed in the fields around town, ranched in the canyon, taught school in the valley, and built and improved the city. His smiling face, quick jokes and gruff farmer voice charmed all the women and befriended all the men he met. He was honest to the core, raised his children to love education and honesty. He even took in stragglers who needed a hand up.

Lynn Jones is one of the many characters who bring people back to Spanish Fork.

GEORGE BEARDALL

You can't miss his house. There are Geese on the lawn. Not real, live geese, but life size, with feathers. George's nickname is "Goose."

There are many people in Spanish Fork, mostly men, who have nicknames. Some have earned theirs; some deserved the names they got. George deserved his name. One day, George ducked out (pun intended) of basketball practice at the high school so he and some buddies could go goose hunting. Coach Gus Black didn't think much of the antics and leveled his displeasure on the one he thought was the perpetrator of the absence. He bestowed the title on George.

So, for the next fifty years, George has been Goose. No last name. Just Goose. Now George has a television show on the local network called "Goose in the Wild."

George has filmed over seventy episodes of "Goose in the Wild." It is one of the most watched shows on Spanish Fork Community Network (SFCN) as of 2014. One of his favourite guests is Rory Ripple who can shoe a horse. "Rory is as solid as a rock and can put real hot shoes right on the horse while on TV camera!" Note that means the camera is filming as Rory is shoeing the horse.

Another interesting guest on the "Goose in the Wild" show has been Brian Burr. Brian makes drums out of Aspen trees. He will use a chain saw to carve drums.

Goose has interviewed professional outdoor guides and display elk bugling.

One other captivating guest on his show was Pattie Richards from Mapleton, Utah. Pattie rescues injured wild birds. When people find an injured bird, they call Pattie and she will gently rescue the fowl, take it home and care for it until it is safe to return it to its habitat. If the bird cannot safely return to the wild, Pattie takes the birds to the elementary school to display for the children.

However, in his real life, George Beardall is still an interesting character in Spanish Fork. He can be seen around town riding his bike. This man is now over sixty-five years old and yet, he rides his bicycle all over town. His trips usually take him from his home to the ballpark. George played baseball and basketball for Spanish Fork High School and has coached baseball for 41 years, unpaid. When he retired from coaching, the Recreation Department retired the Angels team altogether. And don't forget George's long-suffering angel wife who has kept score up in the stifling heat of the score booth, counting each and every ball and strike for just as many years! There were several years George took off, and tried to stay away from the ball field, but not many. To this day, he still can be seen sitting in his lawn chair next to his wife, Valerie, way outside the fence behind second base watching his children and/or grandchildren playing ball.

George tries to talk tough. However, it has been said that he has a soft heart sometimes. One example of this was when George found a garden snake in his yard while he was cutting the lawn. He didn't want to hurt the snake. So he enticed the snake and caught it in a pillow case. He twisted the pillowcase at the top and tossed it on the front seat of his car. Then, he jumped into the car and drove down to the jail. His intention was to let the snake out in that ornamental bubbling brook in front of the Utah County Jail, that way the snake could survive in the wild. However, when George arrived at the jail, he could not find the snake! After an exhaustive search, he finally found the fleeing snake inside the air-conditioning system of his new car! Luckily, he was able to free the errant snake from the inside of his car and into the wild.

As George was returning home to finish his yard work this gave him an environmental idea. It turns out that there were several snakes in George's neighborhood that came looking for their friend, only to also receive a trip to the jail (except, now George had concocted a better mode of transportation for his "guests").

This man is a devoted fan of his family, sports, his religion and this community.

DEAN G. STONE

For a time, Dean was a popular name in Utah. Why, even in the United States! There were actors named Dean. For instance, Dean Jones, Dean Stockwell, the wrestler Dean Ambrose, even Dean Martin the singer/actor/comic/ pretend drunk. Dean Ludlow, Dean Swenson and Dean Sorenson were from Spanish Fork, to name a few. Dean was a favourite name for a while. There was one family I know quite well that had lots of Deans. Alma Stone named his son Dean Alma, who then named his son Dean Alma Jr., whose cousin was named Dean Gordon Stone whose cousin's husband was named Dean Brown and another cousin's husband was Dean Rasmussen. So, to keep it all straight and so they would know who was supposed to help with the dishes they called Dean Alma "D. A." Then they called Dean Gordon, "Dean G." They tried to think of a good nickname for Dean Alma Stone Jr. ("Rockie" was a favorite) but they ended up calling him "Deanie" so he moved away. Dean Brown stayed in Colorado and Dean Rasmussen moved to Arizona for awhile.

One of those many "Deans" was well known in Spanish Fork. He is the one who married Ilene Clayson from Lakeshore. They did not name any of their children "Dean" (though technically, he did name his first son,

"Ricky Dean"), and he ran the Beeline Service Station on Main Street where Zions Bank is now.

Of all the gas stations on Main Street, Don Taylor's Mobile was really popular. One theory was that travelers from California would shop for a certain name brand gas. So they would be drawn to Don Taylor because Mobile Oil was familiar to the California tourists. Dean G. would sit in his station and watch the license plates pull into Don's Mobile. Of course, to give credit where it is due, Don Taylor was an extremely nice guy and a good businessman too.

Dean G. did not stop with just a gas station. He moved into the tire business. He moved to Salt Lake to work for J. C. Penney's where they sold tires along with the gas. That concept really worked for Dean. He was such a born salesman! Dean soon began working for Big O Tires and ended up owning twenty-one stores from San

Diego to Missoula Montana. He and his wife retired and moved back to Spanish Fork. Now, he can comfortably just go by the name of Dean Stone with no competition.

MARIE HUFF

In the United States, in the year 2015, it was not important who you were. It was important what you were. It was important what race, religion, age, sex, culture, or political party you claimed. In Spanish Fork, in 2015, all that just doesn't matter—and never has. As a matter of fact, in 1990 this town elected a woman for

Marie Huff

mayor. This was not just any woman for the sake of the notoriety of saying "We elected a female for mayor." Nor was it for the reason of her age. Marie Huff was elected because she was an accomplished business woman. She had at one time owned and operated a gift shop on Main Street and a restaurant at the base of Spanish Fork Canyon. People would drive from Salt Lake City on Friday nights to the Oak Crest Inn for the Prime Rib and dancing. She sat on city boards like the Arts Council and the Chamber of Commerce. This woman was a mother, a wife, and a power to be reckoned with.

Marie's campaign for mayor was a grassroots effort and organized by former mayor, Dr. Wells Brockbank. Lucky for her that in those days, at least around here, a person's support groups could be organized by each LDS ward list. Wow! What a great calling tree that made. Marie and Dr. Brockbank had political campaign meetings in her home where they assigned ward calling lists to campaign volunteers who eagerly contacted each name on the list and fed them facts and talking points.

Marie Huff was mayor for seven years. Once she brought the circus to town (literally). She even rode an elephant down Main Street! She was an accomplished public speaker who told hilarious stories of days gone by.

When Marie had the gift shop on Main Street, it was always interesting to see what she would set out on the sidewalk by the door. Whatever it was, it enticed people to walk into the store, just to see what was up. Sometimes it could be a large cookie jar. When you peeked in the door you would smell fresh ginger cookies that were the special of that day. Of course while you were waiting for Marie to slowly wrap up the cookies you would wander around the store and…what do you know! There was a perfect gift for some neighbor, friend, sister or some gift you might need in a rush. She was no dummy, nor was she a slow package wrapper. She knew good marketing.

After that, other businesses started putting little teasers of some kind outside or on the door of their stores. While she was on the Chamber of Commerce board she instigated the "Home-cooking Award." This award was given to a local employee who had given exceptional service or displayed a good attitude to customers. The winners were nominated by their employers and then presented with an apple pie from The Oak Crest Inn.

The Oak Crest Inn was a beautiful, sit-down restaurant at the mouth of the Spanish Fork Canyon with a panoramic view of the golf course and the river bottoms. Many people scheduled wedding suppers, class reunions, and special celebrations there. The Rotary Club held their luncheons at the Oak Crest Inn because there were several sections of the dining area that could be closed off for meetings. One room even had a piano if you wanted a program.

When someone went to the restaurant for dinner, they hardly ever had to wait to be seated. Once seated, the servers would bring some of their wonderful soft rolls with honey butter and a tureen of fresh hot soup. Then guests could study the menu, snack on a soft, hot roll smothered in honey butter, and serve themselves a cup of hot vegetable soup. Local people didn't really have to study the menu because they already knew what they would order as soon as they got out of their car and walked over the bridge to the restaurant.

Some ladies' clubs met at the Oak Crest every month. They would be seated in one of the smaller, more private areas in case they had planned a speaker or musical number, (musical numbers were frequently performed by someone's grandchild). The ladies were always dressed up just so.

One unfortunate club luncheon was disturbed by a new young serving girl, who accidentally misjudged the weight of the water pitcher and, missing the glass entirely, poured cold water all over the table, cloth napkins and all. Despite all the hub-bub, the ladies club continued with their lunch and program. They kept having club at the Oak Crest for years.

On another occasion, the Rotary Club was having their weekly luncheon in one of the smaller sections. They had devoured the yummy hot rolls and salad and were just waiting for the main course when they were disturbed by something going on in the next room. The gentlemen stopped eating and started searching around for an explanation of the disturbance. As they listened more closely, the group decided there was some kind of prank going on in the next room and they should all go check it out.

Lead by the president, Richard Roach, who was the branch manager of the Spanish Fork Zions Bank, they all converged on the ruckus in the next room. What they found was a strange man in a Tarzan costume, singing at the top of his voice, "She's FORTY!" while dancing around the long table. The obvious recipient of the saga had her head buried into her napkin. If this had been reported in the Spanish Fork Press, they would have said, "A good time was had by all, but one."

CHAPTER 5:
POLIO IN SPANISH FORK

KATHLEEN BARBER: *December 17, 1934 - August 25, 1949*
DOUGLAS BARBER: *July 21, 1944 - September 4, 2007*

Kathleen and Douglas Barber lived in one of the homes on Eighth North in Little Chicago. This is a section of town where Jex construction built homes all around the square block of 800 North and 700 North between 300 and 400 East. All the homes started out with the same floor plan, and were for the returning soldiers, each home facing the street, thus creating a large square park in the center called for some reason "Little Chicago." You can still see it today, except the homes have been personalized with minor changes to each one.

The Barber's house was *really* clean. Mrs. Barber used the hottest water in the west! She was meticulously clean in all areas. One theory about polio was that some homes were so clean that the children did not create antibodies to fight off infection. This creates a conflict because Mrs. Barber's sole purpose of such cleanliness was to avoid infection. But this is just one theory. However, it has been proven that polio as not caused by playing in the ditch water like everyone thought at the time.

The Barbers had four children who slept in the basement; fourteen-year-old Kathleen, ten-year-old Keith, seven year old Joan and-five-year-old Douglas.

One hot, summer night in August 1949, Kathleen had her cousin Donna sleeping over. Usually, when Donna slept over the girls would giggle late into the night. But this night, they were quiet. Kathleen didn't feel very good, so they went to bed earlier than usual. They woke up early the next morning and Kathleen was running a fever. Levi and Myrtle ran a bathtub of cold water to soak blankets so they could wrap Kathleen in the blanket to break her fever. This was not working.

When Doug woke up also with a fever the parents were very frightened. They called Donna's parents in Ogden and asked them to come pick up their daughter so she would not catch whatever sickness the other two children had. Everyone was so afraid of polio because they didn't know what caused it and how it could spread. Myrtle and Levi set up a routine to keep the tub filled with a cold soaking blanket, a wet blanket on each of the two children and then drying blankets hanging in the basement by the stairs. The fevers would not break.

Late one evening after several fruitless days of the cold wraps they finally took the children down to Dr. Milo Moody's office for a spinal tap which unfortunately indicated the polio virus. So the parents called Crab Mortuary who transported the children to Salt Lake City Children's Hospital because there was no ambulance service in town. Mom and Dad followed in their car. Upon arrival at the hospital, Kathleen and Doug were each placed in iron lung machines to help them breathe.

Levi and Myrtle sat beside them the rest of the night. At 6 a.m. the next morning, the doctors pronounced the death of Kathleen and moved her and her iron lung out of the room. The grief-stricken parents made the long lonely trip back to Spanish Fork. Once there, Myrtle was comforted by her mother who had stayed with the other children and Levi slowly trudged down the stairs to the basement, avoiding the hanging, still damp blankets that were awaiting their turn in the cold tub. With a quiet gentle nudge, Levi awakened and spoke to the children about the death of their sister and the grave illness of their little brother.

When Myrtle returned to the hospital in Salt Lake she was greeted by an anxiously curious, frustrated little boy who was not a bit happy to be locked inside this big noisy tube! He seriously asked his mother, "Where is Kathleen? She was right next to me and she is gone now, where is she? Did they let her out? Why can't I get out?" Doug stayed in the iron lung for two weeks.

The polio that had affected Kathleen was the Bulbar strain that was centered in the throat. Doug's polio virus had attached to his spine, causing it to curve. The curve caused his lungs to be compressed, making it difficult to breathe. The infection in his spine also affected his left hand, making it difficult to move his thumb. When he was finally taken out of the iron lung, he had the first of several surgeries. The first operation was to try to straighten his spine and they put him in a body cast that went from his ankles clear up the back of his head and under his chin.

When he came home from the hospital, his brother (who had assigned himself as "the caregiver in charge") placed Doug on a pile of pillows on the living room floor with some little red plastic bricks. Doug would spend hours building garages and houses. However, he was adamant about only building according to the plans that came with the bricks. He didn't like it when someone tried to deviate from the plans! When the weather warmed up, the family would take Doug outside and prop him up on the lawn by reinforcing his back with a thick balloon stick. This sounds bizarre, but it was a real treat for the little boy to get outside and he was content to watch the cars and trucks come down 800 North. As Doug grew, the body cast pinched and hurt him so much that his dad called the doctor who agreed that they would schedule another surgery and stretch him again before putting him in a new body cast. When Doug heard this he sighed a big sigh of relief and the whole cast cracked down the side!

Doug Barber

Doug had many surgeries to try to improve his back and make more room for his lungs to expand. In each surgery, the doctors would stretch his little body as far as it could go to try to "straighten" him out. Then they would cast it in place. He was usually pretty patient with his situation, but as he grew older, his tolerance was tested, especially by his sister, Joan. Doug would use a thin stick to reach down his neck to scratch the center of his growing back. One day, while lying in his usual position on the floor, propped up by pillows, he asked Joan to hand him the stick because he needed to scratch his itchy back. Joan, as sisters do, occasionally handed Doug the stick, just a tiny bit too far away for him to reach. She continued to tease him until he was able finally to quickly grab the stick and in the same motion, he decked his sister and knocked her out cold.

There were other children in the community that were touched by the polio disease in one form or another. Few children were taken like Kathleen, but many were affected in some way. Many families found ways to manage the damages caused by this virus. One family was the Lewis family whose son John contracted the virus. John's mother rode the bus to Salt Lake every day to see her little boy. When John was deemed well enough to be released and returned home, Mrs. Lewis finally felt confident enough to let John play outside while she watched him. But some of the neighbors were concerned that when Johnny would fall down, Mrs. Lewis would not run to him and help him up. She would sit quietly and encourage him to find a way to get up. This turned out to be his mantra: "When life knocks you down, find a way to get yourself back up."

SHARLENE SCHWARTZ IRVINE'S POLIO STORY

I have had friends and family asking me for years to write the story of my getting polio and of my life with polio. As they keep reminding me, "Once you are gone – the story is gone if you don't write it". Throughout my life I have refused to let polio define me. I've pretty much tried to ignore my handicap as much as possible and just get on with my life. However, I do recognize the value of passing this story down for the generations to come.

As a young child, I can't say that I remember a lot about walking or running before I got polio at age 4. My mother said that I walked at 8 ½ month old and that, according to her," I was faster than a streak of lightening." She tells of how I would throw open the front screen door at Tuttle's Apartments where we lived, and before it could slam shut and my mother realize I was gone, I would be across the street crossing the ditch.

Her good friend and neighbor at Tuttle's apartments was Nedra Swenson. Their daughter Jill (9 months younger that me) was also my friend and playmate. Nedra tells of dressing Jill up every day and setting her out on the front porch. Without fail I would come by and push Jill off the porch. Even back then I was fast and full of it.

I have a few picture of me before getting polio (see pictures below). One of the pictures is of me, standing on the lawn by my Grandma Schwartz' front porch, holding my doll. I have some pictures with my little sister Lana and my mother. Another is a picture of me getting a gift from Santa. The Santa picture would have been taken just a few days before I got polio (see picture). But, for the most part, I was so young when I got polio that it seems like I've had it all of my life.

These are some of the pictures of me before getting polio:

Sharlene, Loa (mother),
Glade (father)

Sharlene, Loa (mother),
Lana (sister)

*Sharlene at
Grandma Schwartz'*

*Sharlene with
her baby doll*

Sharlene

*Sharlene & Lana
(about 4 mo. before Polio)*

Sharlene with Santa a few days before getting Polio

I'm now 65 years old (it is 2014). As I write this story that happened 61 years ago, I find that all of those who would know about my experience of getting polio and how the events of it unfolded are getting older or have passed on. As I talked to my mother, my Aunts Donna and Phyllis, all of their memories of my getting polio are slightly different. They don't always remember the events the same.

On December 12, 1952, about one month after my fourth birthday (on November 11), I came down with polio. This became a great trial in all of our lives. My parents lived in fear and dread of this disease, as many parents did, because at this time there was no vaccine. The disease could cause life-long paralysis or even death. One morning, I became ill - they were sure I had polio. They took me to Dr. Preston Hughes who diagnosed me with strep throat and sent me home.

As they were standing me up to the toilet the next morning, my legs collapsed. I was taken back to the doctor and it was then that the doctor realized it wasn't strep throat but polio. They always felt like it was in Primary that I contracted the polio since approximately eight of us from the group came down with it at about the same time.

The General Hospital in Salt Lake City is where the polio patients were taken back then, so that is where I was taken. My mother tells of leaving Dr. Hughes office after being told I did have polio and I needed to be taken to the General Hospital at once. My father was working a mail delivery route at the time. Donna her sister rode with her to Murray where they were able to find my dad on his mail route and from there they all took me to the General Hospital.

I remember how frightened I was that first night in the hospital all alone. I could hear noises (which I now realize were probably the medical carts being pushed up and down the hall) but at the time I thought it was scary things coming to get me and I was all alone. I stayed in the General Hospital for about one week. Lana, my 2 ½ year old sister, was brought in several days after me with polio but was released after several days. My parents brought us each a doll to comfort us. For some reason I remember liking Lana's doll better than mine (typical children). I cried when Lana got to go home and I had to stay all alone, by myself, without any family.

As an adult, I look back on this time and I don't know how my parents even survived it. They were only 24-25 years old and their only two children were both in the hospital with polio. They did not know what the future for either of us would be. Lana had the type of polio (bulbar) that affects the muscles in the face and neck. It did not affect her lungs. For a time one side of her face was partially paralyzed. When they tried to feed her, a lot of the food would just run out of that side of her mouth. Luckily, the paralysis left her after a few weeks. As an adult, the only side affect you can see is that her mouth pulls slightly down on that side when she cries. However, it did affect a part of her brain that learns reading and she was never able to read well. She was always excellent in math and could remember just about any date and event of importance.

From the General Hospital, I was transferred to the LDS Hospital in Salt Lake City. My mother thinks it was during this transfer that they snuck me home to my grandma and grandpa Swenson's for a few hours to be with the family. My Aunts Donna and Phyllis, who I loved dearly, were also there. My parents had instructed everyone that they were not to cry in front of me. When they brought me in my legs were lifeless and just dangling.

I remember grandma's yellow kitchen table. It had a yellow round booster piece that fit in the center where all of the legs curved in and met. This round piece stood about 6" high and about 12" around. It could be used as a booster on the regular chair seat for small children. They put me on this booster chair and I loved it. We all ate a meal together. It tasted so good after so much hospital food. What I didn't realize at the time, was that at one point most of the adults took turns leaving the room to cry once they could see the damage the polio had done. After an hour or so of visiting, they had leave, in order to check me into the LDS Hospital. I remember being devastated that I had to go back to the hospital and wasn't going to get to stay home. I cried my little heart out all the way back to the hospital. I'm sure, at that point, they were wondering if it had been a mistake to bring me home at all and give me a taste of home and family.

I spent that Christmas plus about three more months in the LDS Hospital. . I remember how upset I was when they wouldn't let me go home for Christmas B I just didn't understand.

My mother remembers driving to SLC every day with a Mrs. Kelch. Her family owned a shoe repair shop in Provo. Both of their husbands had to work and couldn't make the trip to Salt Lake daily so Mrs. Kelch and my mother took turns driving. I had paralytic or spinal polio, which caused paralysis to both of my legs and to a lesser extent my back and abdomen. My legs just hung limply as they carried me around. I also remember trying to sit up in a high sided children's hospital bed. I could sit for a few seconds and then I would fall backwards onto the mattress as I would lose my balance. I no longer had the strength to sit alone. The polio had weakened my back and stomach muscles as well as destroying most of the nerves that ran the muscles in my legs.

At one point when I was in the hospital, my parents and grandparents had Elder Harold B. Lee (who later became the president of The Church or Jesus Christ of Latter-day Saints) come in and give me a priesthood blessing. In the blessing he blessed me that I would walk again (even though the doctors said I would be confined to a wheelchair for the rest of my life), and be able to live a happy, normal, productive live. After the blessing he told my parents and grandparents that it did not come to him to say I would be made well. He said that is not the Lords' purpose for her. However, I was able to walk with the aid of crutches and leg braces that went to the top of my legs. I could even walk around the house without the crutches and braces if I could reach out and touch or hold on to something every so often.

I did grow and develop normally (except for the paralysis from the polio and the distortions it caused).

I have made many friends throughout my life that have enriched my life greatly. I attended college at BYU where I graduated in Home Economics Education (now called Family and Consumer Science), married, gave birth to and raised four children (twin sons and two daughters –Jason, Justin, Ashlie and Whitney) and taught school at the Spanish Fork Junior High School for eight years after my own kids were in school. I feel that President Lee's blessing has been fulfilled. I have lived a very full, happy and contented life.

Going back to my childhood, eventually, I was released from the LDS Hospital. I have no memory of this next part, but mother has told me how ever morning and night she was instructed to exercise my legs for one hour. She said I hated this and cried most of the time. However, she didn't dare not do the exercises for fear that if there was any hope of gaining muscles back it would be lost if she failed to do the exercises.

When I was re-learning to walk after the polio, I found it easiest to walk on all fours. With the aid of my arms as a second set of legs, I could travel fairly fast. This was my favorite way to get around inside of the house. Out in public I used the crutches and braces. I walked like this until I was about seven years old. I credit my grandma Schwartz with putting an end to this and making me walk in a more acceptable manner. In a loving way, she told me I wasn't an animal and I needed to walk on just my legs and not all fours. As I grew older, I was thankful that she had encouraged me to do this. I'm sure I looked more normal on two legs than on both legs and hands.

I had my first surgery on my legs at about the age of five. It was performed by a Dr. Kazarian. During this surgery, he fused some of the bones together in my left foot to keep it from rotating inward as my arch was giving away and my weight was shifting to the inside of the foot.

At about this time, my parents and grandpa and grandma Swenson were approached by a Mr. Fred Ray who belonged to the "Shriners". He asked if he could sponsor me. Their organization ran the Shriners Hospital in Salt Lake City. At the time, this children's hospital was one of the biggest and best in the western US. It was a hard decision for my parents. They would be turning over all medical decision making to the Shriners' hospital doctors. The doctors would be determining what was best for me and what surgeries I was to have instead of my parents. On the positive side, they were well known for their excellent doctors and care. In addition, they would pay for all my medical expenses, insuring that I would get excellent care and the best available treatment. My parents finally decided that going with the Shriner's Hospital, would be the very best thing they could do for me. I feel that it was through the gifted hands of these doctors (especially Dr. Coleman), that President Lee's blessing to walk again was fulfilled.

My first surgeries at Shriners Hospital were under the direction of a Dr. Lamb but later Dr. Sherman S. Coleman became the head surgeon over the Shriners' Hospital. (Later, he became the head surgeon over orthopedics at the University of Utah hospital as well.) He was a brilliant doctor who was well known throughout the US for his expertise. I have always felt that it was through his hands and knowledge that the Lord fulfilled His blessing that I would walk and have a full normal life. When I first came down with the polio, and my legs dangled limply as they carried me, I was told I would be confine to a wheelchair for the rest of my life. I didn't even own a wheelchair until I was about 35 years old. However, I was forced to use a wheelchair during the recovery from my many surgeries, but I was not confined to a wheelchair once the healing was done.

From age 5 to 14 or 15, I had 21 surgeries on my legs performed by Dr. Sherman S. Coleman. Sometimes it took more than one surgery to accomplish what they wanted. With each surgery, I spent about three months in a cast (at the Shriners hospital) and then had to go through physical therapy to rehabilitate the leg that was operated on. The following are some of the things they did during the surgeries:

This first surgery was the only surgery not performed at Shriners Hospital. They tried to correct the fallen arch in my left foot by fusing the bones. Shortly after getting the cast off my foot, my mother was pushing me in a stroller and my foot fell off the stroller foot rest and was run over. Everyone was so upset for fear they had undone the surgery.

I had both ankles fused so they wouldn't turn from side to side but they left the ankle joints so my feet would go up and down. It was during these surgeries that they placed two screws in each foot. After three month in casts, the bones had grown around these screws and it was extremely painful to have the screwed removed.

They fused the bones in the joints of my big toes so they wouldn't curl under. During this surgery they put about 3" long pins down through the center of the bones in each big toe. The pins stuck out of the tops of my toes about ¼". Both feet were in casts.

They took the muscles that did work to pull my toes up and re-routed the muscles to push my toes down. This helped with my ability to balance myself when walking. Later it helped in driving a car, as I was able to push on the gas and brake pedals.

They also did surgeries to re-route the muscles to pull my feet up so they wouldn't drop when I walked. I was young enough that I don't remember these surgeries well.

On my left leg, they took what little hamstring muscles that still worked in the back of my knee, (used to bend the knee backwards) and re-routed it to the front of the knee. The idea was to help hold my knee straight and keep my leg from collapsing at the knee when I put weight on the leg. However, they routed the muscle from the back and around the <u>outside</u> of the leg to the front of the knee. After healing for three months in a cast, the cast was removed. As physical therapy progressed, they could see that every time I bent my leg, my knee cap flipped out of place and off to the outside of my leg. Leaving an indent where the knee cap should have been. They did a second surgery on my left leg and this time they re-routed the hamstring muscle from the back of the knee and around the <u>inside</u> of my leg and attached it to the front of the knee. I spent another three months healing in a cast and going through physical therapy, but this time the surgery worked and my knee cap stayed in place when I bent the knee. This surgery helped tremendously and made it possible for me to stand without my knee collapsing forward.

After figuring out the best way to re-route the hamstring muscles, they performed the same surgery on my right leg. I didn't have as much working muscle in my right leg so the surgery didn't stabilize that leg as well.

My right leg started to bow out at the knee (see picture). It looked a lot like an extremely bowlegged cowboys leg would look. They broke the femur (upper leg bone) surgically and took a pie shaped wedge of bone out of it so they could bring the leg into a straight position. This also helped the leg so it didn't bow backwards. When a leg bows backwards, it looks like the knee is bending in the opposite direction than what it should – backwards. (My left leg still bows backwards and has since I was small). They placed an "L" shaped piece of metal down the outside of the bone and through the bottom of the bone just above the knee. This metal plate was held in place with three long screws. The bottom part of the "L" stuck out about ¼" further than the bone on the inside of my right knee.

For this surgery, they wrapped me in a solid cast that went from under my arm pits down to the top of my legs and continued down my entire right leg including my foot. I was stuck in a permanent laying position for 5 months. While in this cast, they operated on my left leg. The day after this surgery the "Blue Angles" stunt flying group made a visit to Shriners' hospital. I was still in bed and in a lot of pain but they took my picture with the "Blue Angles" standing around the bed (see picture). An article and this picture were put in the newspaper telling about their visit. It was during this time that they kept me in the hospital for five months and I didn't get to see my new baby brother Randy until he was three months old. The physical therapy after this surgery was very extensive and painful as they had to rehabilitate and strengthen the hip, knee and ankle joints as well as my back and abdomen.

Several years after having the "L" shaped metal plate put into my right leg; the nerves grew over the part of the plate that was sticking out past my bone at the knee. This area became extremely painful if touched. The doctors felt like the bone had healed and was strong enough that they could remove the "L" shaped plate and give me some relief from the pain. They did remove the plate but they had to saw off the heads of the three screws attaching the plate to the femur bone because they couldn't get the screws out of the bone.

Within about five to six years after having the plate removed from my right leg, the leg started to bow out again (see pictures before and after the right leg was surgically broken and straightened). The bowing was so bad that I could stand with my knees together and my right foot would extend over (or swing around) so I could place my right foot on the outside of my left foot as I stood. By now (1968) I was 18 years old and had finished my freshman year at BYU. For a second time, I had to have the femur bone of the right leg re-broken and another pie shaped piece of bone removed from the leg to straighten it out. They put another "L" shaped plate in the leg and once again it stuck out about ¼" to ½" past the bone on the inside just above the knee. The nerves have grown over the plate again but they are not quite as painful as they were with the first plate. It's about 47 years later and I still have this plate in place. This surgery was also performed by Dr. Sherman Coleman.

Needless to say, from the age of about five until the age of fourteen or fifteen, I spent a great deal of time at Shriners being operated on. Dr. Coleman preformed about twenty one surgeries on my legs during this period.

I was blessed that the expertise to perform these surgeries was available in Salt Lake City. If I had been born outside the US, and contracted polio, most likely doctors overseas would not have been able to help me much.

I don't remember all of the surgeries I had but the above surgeries stand out in my mind. However, I do have quite a few memories from my time spent at Shriners. I remember what I think was the first time I arrived at the hospital. I was examined down stairs on the main floor and then later taken up to the second floor where all the children's wards were.

They had all the girl's wards on one end of the hospital and all the boy's wards on the other end. The girls and the boys sections each had three wards B the "Baby Ward" - probably from birth to about five, the ASmall or Little Ward" B from about ages six to ten, and the " Big Ward" B from ages eleven to sixteen. They didn't take kids after age sixteen. I remember how upset I was when they forced my parents to leave and they kept me there that first day. This was made worse by the fact that parents were only allowed to visit for two hours on Sundays. Visitors, other than parents, weren't allowed at all. I think they did this because most kids were from out of state and it made them homesick when they didn't get any visitors. My parents came faithfully every Sunday from 2-4 pm. They owned Glade's Drive Inn by the time I was ten years old and every time they came they would sneak in a big sack of candy. During the week I kept it hidden from the nurses and I would share it with all of my friends. This made it so everyone looked forward to my parents' Sunday visits.

I don't remember a lot about the time I spent in the "small or little" ward. However, I do remember a time when the doctor (not Dr. Coleman but a resident) told me he would ground me to my bed if I picked a certain scab on the side of my face. I think this picking is a genetic thing - I have two aunts, a sister and at least one child that loves to pick at anything that isn't smooth or flat on their skin. Anyway, I had to stay in bed for two days for picking. This same doctor took it upon himself to correct my Spanish Fork English. He was forever correcting my "done" and "did" as I spoke.

After one particular surgery during this time, I remember how badly my leg hurt. It was in a cast from below the knee to the tops of my toes. I was sure, in my delirious state, as I was coming out of the ether, that the leg was something in my bed hurting me instead of being part of me. Even as a child, I had extremely strong arms from all the time I spent using crutches, so

I tried to pick this leg up and throw it out of my bed. It slammed into the rail on the side of the bed so hard that it cracked or dented the cast and caused the incision to bleed. They were quite concerned that they would have to go back in and redo part of the surgery. Luckily, everything turned out OK and the surgery didn't need to be redone.

My mother tells of how parents were not allowed at the hospital during the surgeries. She said she remembered being home mowing the lawn and bawling because she knew I was in surgery and she wasn't allowed to be there. They must have let parents in after the surgery was finished, because she was there when I tried to throw my leg out of the bed. I also remember her pulling my toes forward in the cast. For some reason that made my whole leg feel better.

During one of my many hospital stays, (usually most summers and occasionally during the school year) they fused both of my ankle joints so my feet could move up and down but not from side to side. This was done to keep me from walking on the outside of my right foot and the inside of my left foot. During the surgery, they had placed two screws in each foot. (This was mentioned briefly before). One screw from the center top of the foot and one screw from the center bottom of the foot, both angled in toward the center of the foot and ankle joint. After the bones had mended, it was time to take the casts off and remove the screws. I was only about eight or nine at the time and hated the saw that removed the casts. I'm sure this had something to do with the fact that after three month of wearing a particular cast, I had most of the cotton pulled out of it. I did this so I could stick things inside the cast and scratch all of the spots that itched.

They removed the cast, and then it was time to remove the four screws. They gave me nothing to numb my feet but proceeded to attach a hand drill to the screws. They unscrew the four screws (two in each foot) from the bones of each foot. I remember screaming from the pain and trying to pull away, and them trying to hold me down and telling me not to act like a baby. Normally, they were very kind and caring people, so I still don't understand why they did it that way.

During another surgery, I had pins placed down through the centers of both of my big toes. The toe joints had been fused to keep my toes from curling under. Having those pins removed wasn't nearly as traumatic. The toe pins were smooth on the sides so they came out fairly easily. They just grabbed hold of the pins and pulled hard and they came out. However, the screws into my ankles were threaded all around like actual screws, so the bone had grown around them and into the threading. They literally had to be unscrewed like a screw in wood. It was extremely painful and really, really hurt when they were removed.

The doctors performed many surgeries in which they took part of a good muscle and re-routed it to take the place, or at least help out where a muscle had been completely paralyzed. They did this on my feet and then later on my knees. It always amazed me how the brain could figure this out how to make the muscle perform a new function. You could take a muscle designed to do one thing, move one end of it to a new location, and the muscle or brain would know to do something else. I do think they had to leave it attached at one end though. They couldn't just take the whole muscle out and move it to some other part of the body.

I remember them filming me at Shriners' Hospital, as I would walk ten or twenty feet without the use of crutches or braces. They considered it amazing that I could walk at all with as little muscle as I had left in my legs.

I wore full length leg braces (or at least I was supposed to wear them) for walking from the time I was five until I was about fifteen or sixteen. These braces attached to the bottom of my shoes. They had stainless steel bars that ran up the outsides of my legs with half circle metal bands, covered in leather, in several places in the back between the bars. These ran to the tops of my legs where the leather bands wrapped around to the front and buckled to hold the braces in place. I could walk without the braces but the doctors made me wear them because they were afraid my bones would grow crooked because they had so little muscle and ligaments to support them.

When I was younger the doctors tried to make me wear a back brace with steel supports to keep my back straight. I really hated it, because it dug in everywhere. I was constantly taking it off. As a result, of not wearing the brace, my back is somewhat crooked B but not bad. At age fourteen (I was becoming a vain teenager) I took the leg braces off and refused to wear them. By age 19, my right leg had started to bow to the outside again and I had to have the femur bone re-broken, straightened and a new plate put in the leg to keep the bone straight. I later went back into the full length leg braces after giving birth to twins and still continue to wear them. I have always used the crutches when walking outside but not in the house.

There were several unpleasant or difficult things I remember about being at Shriners. As a child I had had so many surgeries that I would get emotionally stressed and feel ill whenever I smelled alcohol because I associated it with surgery and the operating room.

I hated having casts removed. I was always sure the cast saw would cut my leg. After wearing a cast for several months, I usually had most of the cotton pulled out, once during the cast removal the saw did scrape up my leg and caused it to bleed because of this. Once a cast was removed, my leg looked and felt so foreign. It looked pale, soft and lifeless with no muscle structure. It would have black hairs from lack of sun and tons of dead skin that would peel off. At this point they would send me down to the big Hubbard Tank which was about twice the size of a hot tub. It had swirling water like a hot tub but much more gentle. This is where they would start the rehabilitation process. Then they would send you the dreaded physical therapists. If you were in a bent leg cast they would force your leg to straighten out and if you were in a straight leg cast they would force the leg to bend. This was extremely painful. I remember coming right up out of my wheelchair on many occasions as I went through this process over and over again.

We all hoped and prayed we were not in the hospital when the dentists showed up. For some reason they did not give shots to numb the teeth as they worked on them. This was pure torture. No one (especially children) wants to have their teeth drilled into without anything for pain. As I said earlier, for the most part these were wonderful and kind people that ran the hospital. I still don't understand why they had dentists that came in and filled teeth without giving something for pain.

I have many happy memories from my days at Shriners' also. Once I was old enough to be in the "Big Ward" I really didn't mind being in the hospital.

For some reason they didn't run the Shriners' Hospital like other hospitals and especially like hospitals today. Now, you go in for surgery, and either leave the same day or stay overnight to a few days. The healing is done at home. At Shriners, you had the surgery, stayed in the hospital until the healing process was completed, the cast removed, and physical therapy finished. This would usually take three months or more depending on what they did to you. On one stay, they kept me in the hospital for five months straight. However, after the initial pain from the surgery ended, they got me up and out of bed every day. This was standard practice for all patients. They brought clothes racks around every morning after our bed baths and we got to pick which dress we wanted to wear that day. We only wore hospital gowns after surgery.

We were then placed in a wheelchair, or "cripple-cart" (see picture) as we called them. The "cripple cart" was a long wooden boxed sort of thing with four inch high sides all around. It had two big wheelchair type wheels on the front end so we could wheel ourselves where we wanted to go. These were used for patients that couldn't sit up. This is what I used when I had the full body cast around my middle and down my right leg. They placed a slanted bolster at the end with the big wheels or where your head was. This made it possible for kids with body casts (from spinal surgery) or kids like me who couldn't sit because of full length body casts, to wheel themselves around as they were in a partial laying position (I have pictures of me in one).

Because we were not forced to stay in bed, life seemed fairly normal. We attended school in a large school room with the boys during the school year. They had crafts, puppet shows etc. in the "sunroom" and on good days during the summer, they would take all those that could go, outside. We even had a circus that came once a year. All in all, it was more like living in a big dorm with all your friends than it was like a hospital. On one occasion, when I was older, I even cried when I had to go home and leave all my friends. However, there were many occasions, like when my baby brother Randy was born and I couldn't go home and see him that I cried because I had to stay.

There was one nurse at the hospital whose last name was Engebretsen. She let us call her Engie for short. I just loved her. She made life so much better for all of us. She was fun and friendly and you could tell how much she cared for each of us. We always looked forward to when she worked.

I need to stop here and explain the set-up of the "Big Ward" in order for everything to make sense. It was like a large spoke or finger that jutted out from the main body of the hospital. It had windows on the two long sides of the room and the outer end was a " sunroom" with windows all around it. (That is where we ate our meals, did crafts and various other activities.) Most of the way down the center of the long room was a six foot high partition. This partition had lights and nightstands for each of the six or eight beds that had their headboards up against it and going down both sides of the partition. The feet of the beds were facing the outside walls with all the windows.

There was an eight foot wide area to walk all the way around the outside of the room between the beds and the windows. You could walk into the sunroom from either side of the room, forming a large long oval walkway around the room and the beds. From the beds, you had a panoramic view of the outside world. On the left end of the long room, there was a smaller room that contained the bed pans with a large hose used to clean them. The room also contained several toilets in stalls for those that could walk and sinks for washing hands. On at least one occasion several of us had a water fight in that room using the hoses and water from the sinks. Needless to say, we were grounded to our beds for the next day.

On other occasions, we had wheelchair races in the "big" room because it formed a long oval when we went through the "sunroom" and back up the other side. Because most of us weren't "sick" but recovering, and healing from surgeries, we didn't need constant care. The nurses spent more of their time in the "Baby Ward" and the "Small Ward". One night after the nurses had finished getting everyone to bed and had left to attend to charts or whatever they did, several of us got out of bed. We had taken plastic water bottles that we had filled with water and hidden earlier during the day. That night we had a huge water fight. We had to scoot on the floors under the beds to get around because all of our wheelchairs had been taken to the sunroom to be stored for the night. Luckily we didn't get caught.

Later, during my early teen years, I had what I thought of as a "boyfriend" from the boys group of patients. The only time we got to see each other was during school or when we were all taken outside together.

We were not allowed to have make-up in the hospital; so several of us that were teenagers and trying to impress the boys, took up using our school pencils as eye liner. We painted it on the inside bottom edges of our eye just above the eyelashes. As you can well imagine, the doctors had a fit over this when they found out. None of us knew anything about lead poising but the doctors did. They explained about lead poising and threatened severe consequences if we did it again.

During my time at Shriners, I had a friend named Theresa (see picture). She had polio in her back and was in an upper body cast after having surgery on her back. We became such good friends that I was invited to her home in Hawthorn, Nevada where I stayed a week or two. Her legs had some weakness but they had enough muscles that they were shaped like legs but just a little thinner. She had a doctor (not from Shriners) that told her not to walk on her legs unless she had braces on, so she hardly ever walked. When we were about 55 years old she was in Utah and looked me up and we all went to dinner. She had used her legs very little over the years. They were not bent out of shape (like mine are) from use, but I was still walking and she was completely confined to a wheelchair. I was glad I had used my legs as much as I could before they wore out.

Sharlene 6 ½ yrs with long leg braces. Loa Pregnant with Randy

Great grandpa Albert Swenson, Grandpa Harold Swenson with Sharlene, Loa & Lana

Sharlene 6 ½ yrs. In a
cast after surgery

Lana and Sharlene
(about 8-9 yrs.old)

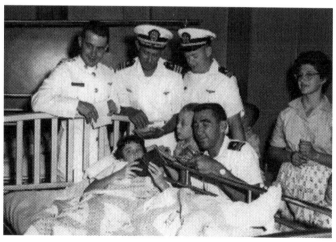

Sharlene (the day after knee surgery on my L
knee) with the Blue Angels Flying Group

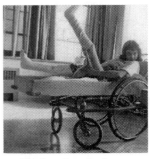

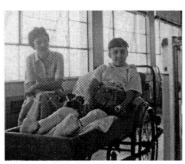

Sharlene in cripple-cart
showing knee scar-12yrs.

Sharlene Sunday visiting
hours with Loa

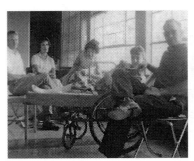

Visiting hrs. with Sharlene&
best friend Threase

Sharlene with new long
leg braces 14 yrs.old

*Sharlene 1967 Sr. Year –***before** *R leg was Surgically broken and straightened*

Sharlene 1970-71
after *R leg was surgically broken and straightened*

Because my paralysis was so extensive, it has been the root of other problems throughout my life. In addition to the 21 surgeries on my legs during my childhood, I have had many other surgeries because of the weakness caused by polio. I have had to have the following additional surgeries:

All four of my children were delivered C-section because my back was crooked and my abdominal muscles were week. The first children were twin boys (Jason and Justin), the third and fourth were girls (Ashlie and Whitney).

After Whitney, my fourth and last child was born; I had to have my abdominal wall completely reconstructed.

Going into the surgery, the doctor had discussed doing the surgery a certain way. After surgery, the doctor (Clifford Snyder) came to the room and told me everything had fallen into place to perform the surgery using a completely different procedure. He felt that he had been guided in doing the surgery a different way, as the muscle and fascia (muscle covering) had been in place for him to perform the surgery differently.

The day after surgery, I was given a priesthood blessing and anointing by two missionaries making rounds at the University of Utah Hospital. When they arrived at my room, they asked if I would like a blessing. I told them I had had one before having surgery but I was sure another one couldn't hurt. In this blessing, I was told that with this surgery, I had been given a miracle from the Lord and it should be recognized as such. Before this surgery my stomach muscles had been torn apart from having the twins (Justin was 5lbs. 13oz. and Jason was 5lbs. 8oz.). The abdominal muscle wall was torn from the pubic bone on the bottom to the rib cage on top. I looked 6 months pregnant all the time. This lack of muscle support had allowed my back to arch forward, causing almost continuous muscle spasms in my back. After this surgery, everything was pulled back into place and is still holding 28 years later. My back muscles will tighten at times but I no longer have the muscles spasms I was having before the surgery. It truly was a miracle from the Lord.

Also, because polio weakened the muscles in my body core, after all my children were born, they had to repair a lot of the structure in the abdominal and pelvic area.

When Whitney was in first grade and the boys were getting ready to leave on missions, I started teaching Family and Consumer Science classes at the Spanish Fork Jr. High School. One of the classes that I taught was sewing. I taught for eight years. However, in 2001, at the age of 53, I tore the rotator cuffs in my shoulders. My arms had been so unbelievably strong, after using crutches for 49 years, that I would have thought this was impossible. But eventually, I just started wearing my shoulders out. I thought I would go in, have the surgery to repair the shoulder, and be back to work in several weeks. I had no idea I could be so wrong! This surgery completely changed my life. I went from being paraplegic to quadriplegic overnight. My left arm was the only limb that worked at all. I quickly found that with only one arm, I couldn't stand myself up, get in and out of a chair or bed, get on or off a toilet or in or out of a tub. About the only thing I could do was feed myself, and even then I had to have help cutting up food.

Everywhere I went I had to be hoisted in a Hoyer lift. (Much like the lifts they use to remove an engine from a car). Jay and my parents were wonderful at helping me through this. Every day, my parents came and took me out to lunch just to get me out of the house. (This meant we often had to haul the Hoyer lift in the back of my van in order to get me in and out of the wheelchair. After this surgery I was forced to use an electric wheelchair. As it turned out, I would use the electric wheelchair around the house from then on and a manual wheelchair if I left the house. Both of my arms were so weakened from this surgery I never recovered enough strength to use crutches as my main mode of transportation. Also, my knee joints had become so worn that walking was uncomfortable.

Because my left arm was the only limb that worked after the rotator cuff surgery, I over stressed that arm, especially the elbow joint. I have had two surgeries on that elbow to remove bone spurs caused by the excess stress. After one of the surgeries, I was given too much prednisone; the stitches pulled apart exposing the bone and elbow joint. It had to be healed as an open wound. The wound had to be packed twice daily by a nurse and three times a week I had to have a whirlpool bath treatment on it. This lasted for three months. At the end of the three months, the skin had pulled together unevenly and left a terrible scar which they finally had to go in and revise during a third surgery.

It was during my first elbow surgery, that I was given a combination of drugs, while I was anesthetized, that I reacted to. This surgery was supposed to be same day surgery. However, my body temperature dropped to such a low level during surgery, that they had to place me in a body bag (the type they put you in once you have died) and blow hot air into it for hours, in order to bring by body temperature back up. I had to stay the night in the hospital because I would breathe out and then not take another breath. I would lay there for a long period of time and then gasp for air.

Jay was in my hospital room until late at night and had to keep reminding me to breathe in. It seemed that I had lost that automatic breathing reflex. I had no saliva for 36 hours and the whole underside of my arm from the arm pit to the wrist turned black from excess blood drainage. It swelled to a much larger size than the other arm and was extremely tight and uncomfortable feeling. As they removed the bone spur, they thought a small piece of the bone had chipped off, which nicked the artery or some other blood vessel.

Later that night when I finally warmed up I asked the nurse if they could remove the body bag. She said she had seen the bag but didn't dare say anything about it until she found out what had gone wrong and why I was in it.

As an adult (and at the time of this writing December 2014) I've had about 23 surgeries (in addition to the ones I had on my legs as a child) but the above 11 procedure were brought on because of polio and the damage it caused. I am 66 years old and so far I've had 44 surgeries.

When I was given the blessing by President Harold B Lee, when I first got polio, he blessed me that I would have good people to befriend and help me through this life and my trials. I consider this to be a great blessing in my life; one of the tender mercies from the Lord.

As an adult, one of my greatest blessings has been my husband Jay. He has quietly stood by me throughout the many surgeries and trials I have had as an adult. He has been a great help and support throughout our married life. We were blessed with two sons (twins) and two daughters. All of them have learned many lessons because of my handicap. They have grown up to be good, caring, compassionate people.

Through my early years, I was blessed with wonderful friends. Pat Kempton and Robin Sanford were friends that I made in grade school. As we entered Junior High school and High School, both of them made arrangements to take classes with me so they could carry my books from class to class. Jill Swenson was a friend and cousin that I've known since we were one or two years old. In college, my good friends were Janet Howard (Bauer), Fae Perry (Herlocker), and Celia Gresko (Palmer). Celia and I have remained close for over 45 years. She lives a few houses from me now and all of our children were raised almost like brothers and sisters. I have also kept in touch will all of my roommates -Lindy, Aleen, Bonnie, Sue P. and Sue from my freshman year at BYU, when we lived in Fox Hall. I have had so many people bless and enrich my life.

I was blesses with wonderful parents (Glade and Loa Jean Swenson Schwartz) and grandparents (Harold and Jen Swenson and Ida Schwartz Hall). My grandpa Paul Schwartz died when I was two but Grandma Schwartz later married Dan Hall who was like a grandpa. My parents always made me feel like I was capable of doing anything I set my mind to and never tried to pamper me or pity me. For this reason I grew up being very independent, feeling like I could do or accomplish anything I set my mind to. I did not grow up feeling "handicapped". My Grandma Swenson once said to me when I was about eight, "The Lord must love you an awful lot to give you such a big trial in life. You must be very special". This changed my whole perspective on having polio and a handicap. I no longer felt picked on or unlucky – I felt special and privileged. I have a strong belief in the Lord. I have felt Him by my side on many, many occasions as I have gone through this journey.

As a young child, I felt sure I couldn't have a surgery without my Grandpa Harold Swenson and my dad giving me a priesthood blessing. Once I had the blessing, I was sure everything would turn out all right. As an adult, I have been given many priesthood blessings by my father (Glade Schwartz), my husband (Jay Irvine) and my sons (Jason and Justin Irvine). I am so thankful and blessed to be surrounded by worth priesthood holders. I have a strong testimony and belief in the power of prayer and the power of the priesthood. I believe everyone is called upon to go through trials in this life. Having polio gave me the opportunity to learn principles that I would never have otherwise learned. I am so thankful the Lord gave me the opportunity to learn these lessons. This life is a time of testing and proving. I believe it is the attitude we take, how we handle, and what we do with the trials we are given that determines the person we will become.

CHAPTER 6: STORIES

FIRST RESPONDERS DESERVE OUR THANKS
Mayors of Utah County—Provo Daily Herald; Mayor Leifson

Recently, Spanish Fork experienced two public emergencies; a house fire and a very dramatic rescue of a beautiful little girl. I appreciate this forum where I can publicly address issues such as this. Today, I publicly thank those who have chosen to serve our communities as first responders. Their service is vital to our welfare, and often their efforts go unnoticed. That may be how they want it, but every once in awhile I think we all need to express our appreciation to those who respond to an emergency call.

These events remind me that responding to emergences requires many different people to work seamlessly together. There are some who may do one job or another task, but everyone collectively does the thing that contributes to the overall success of the response. Thanking any one individual or group would not be appropriate as they all deserve our gratitude.

In March of 2015, Spanish Fork first responders made national news with an amazing rescue experience.

A young mother accidentally hit a cement guard rail at the junction of Arrowhead Trail and Highway 189 late at night, knocking her car off the road and into the Spanish Fork River, upside down. The young mother was killed. The following day a fisherman noticed the upturned car and called 911. The first responders arrived and approached the car with rescue equipment. Officer Bryan Dewitt went down into the cold river water and took sad note of the passing of the twenty-five year- old driver of the car. Fire Chief Brent Jarvis arrived and they began assessing the plan necessary to upright the vehicle.

When Officers Warner, Beddoes and Harward arrived they put the plan into motion. The three officers with the assistance of Officer Dewitt and the fisherman got into the 32 degree, icy cold water to carefully upright the partially submerged mid-sized car. The cold winter breeze rushed over the cold river water. As they did so, they all heard a soft female voice cry out, "Help us!" With Fireman Tyson Shepherd standing in the freezing river water balancing the car so it wouldn't tip, Firemen

Lee Mecham, Allen Moore and Paul Tomadakis got the door open.

Firefighter Paul Tomadakis cut the straps that held the child's car seat, and carefully lifted her tiny eighteen-month-old body out of the near freezing water and handed her to the awaiting officers who tenderly reached up the riverbank and passed the fragile baby clad only in a thin flannel onesie to each other, beginning with Lee Mecham, then to Officer Dewitt, who then passed her to Officer Beddoes who finally passed her further up the river bank to Officer Warner. Officer Warner, being the last in the chain of brave, cold, rescuers, ran with the baby to the awaiting ambulance and its crew, Nina Mortensen, Mark Byers, and Erika Nielsen, and administered CPR while en route to the hospital. The ambulance rushed her to the Payson Hospital where their emergency team placed her in the Life Flight Helicopter and took off for Primary Children's Hospital in Salt Lake City. The little girl named Lilly survived her encounter in spite of spending a long, lonely night hanging upside-down in freezing water nearly up to her chin. Three police officers and four firefighters were treated that day for hypothermia.

The Utah State Department of Emergency Services presented the Spanish Fork Police, Fire and Ambulance Crews with the "Outstanding Call of the Year" award.

Even on NBC's Today Show, the news anchor expressed his amazement that "no matter what your beliefs, this was a miracle." And it happened in Spanish Fork.

SOMEONE NEW

I quit California. Left all the fires, ash, soot, cars, movie stars, fake movie stars, wanna-be-movie stars. I had no family there and no close friends. I'm pretty sure I won't be missed.

I got as far as the middle of Utah, some Podunk town full of cowboys, cable guy lookalikes, soccer moms, baseball fields and a million church steeples. And between all the baseball fields and the churches, I must have seen a zillion kids of all ages playing soccer. What was this place?

As I drove around the neighborhoods I saw clean streets, mowed and trimmed lawns, fenced-in back yards and lots of flags in the front yards. Some of the flags were solid red with a big U on them and some were blue and white with BYU on them. I even saw American flags of all kinds, some as yard art, made out of wooden pallets or old interior doors. At the beginning and the very end of the Main Street there were huge American flags.

As I was driving into town I also saw a huge fairground with a really amazing rodeo arena and just south of Main Street I saw several huge baseball fields with tons of parking around them. *Geez*, I thought, *does anyone here work or do they just play ball, ride horses and go to church?*

Just out of curiosity, I turned around at the north end of town and went back up Main Street to look at the little shops along the way. I saw a big tire store that looked like it could have once been a grocery store and an insurance office that could have been a bank, maybe in the seventies. I really liked to see what had once been really old businesses or stores that had been fixed up and refurbished and used now as beauty shops or antique stores. So, I pulled to the curb and decided to go into the drug store and get some aspirin. I hoped maybe they'd have a cold drink machine to wash it down with.

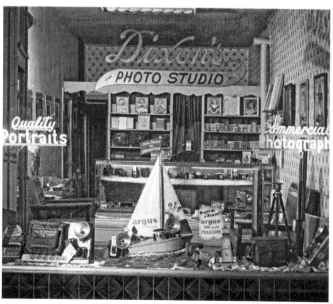

235

Boy was I surprised! It was a real pharmacy, sure, but it was also a book store, gift store, and school supply store. In one stop, I could get the aspirin I went in for, but I could also pick out greeting cards, wheelchairs if I had a mind, pencils, pens, crayons and candy. As I looked around, there was no cold drink machine! What? Then I saw the grill and smelled the burgers and fries. Smart stop, I congratulated myself. I sat down on the ancient round stool reminiscent of the old soda fountain stools, and ordered the "special" cheeseburger, fries and a Coke. I could even have had a cherry Coke but at the time I was into the nostalgia versus modern era mode, so I went with the pure, unadulterated Coke.

While I sat at the counter savoring my lunch "special," I listened to the other people as they came into the store. I thought they were speaking a form of the English language I hadn't heard before. One person asked for directions and the other person who must have been some form of a preacher said "Go forth and see the place by where the big spruce ustabe, by where them ole fire trucks was... no, hold on, flip a u-ie jest past jay mark where the ol' Christians was and by the Mexican place by what couldah been Don Taylor's Mobile." Hmmm. I wasn't even going to try to follow that advice.

However, I also noticed that when people would come into the store they were greeted by friends and neighbors, I guess, who acted first like they were long lost friends who needed to catch up on children and illnesses, and then like they were reporters from the local Fox News. They exchanged gossip about the comings and goings of the townspeople, the ball games and the next election. Apparently, everyone knew something about somebody or some event and was glad to share.

It was then that I decided to investigate how I could become a piece of this interesting quilt made up of friends, schoolmates, relatives and neighbors. I wondered if it would be possible to fit in at all. One thought I had was that I needed to marry someone from this town in hopes of becoming a proxymember who would always be referred to as "that Californian who married that kid we went to school with."

I knew that would never happen in my lifetime, so I went out, got into my car, turned around, and headed north. But as I traveled farther north, nothing was the same, not really. Yes, there were some ball fields and lots of churches, and kids. Really! I saw tons of little kids in every town. Now, I figured out what else they do around here besides baseball. However, when considering the similarities in all the small towns, the one town with the rodeo ground, flags, and the drug store still held sway.

So, I made a decision. I turned my car around and headed south, back to that small town. This time, I stopped just inside the town at the big grocery store. I went in, met the store manager, immediately filled out some paperwork, left my short resume and then hit the bakery aisle for treats. On my way to the bakery (I could have just followed the sweet smells), a young store employee asked me if I needed any help. When I told her what I was looking for, she didn't point me in the right direction. She walked right beside me all the way and just chatted me up. "New in town? Where you from? How long will you be staying?" She acted just delighted when I told her I had just applied for a job at the store and was thinking of staying in town for awhile.

Well, when she heard that I was going to stay she began talking even faster about her aunt's sister's husband who had a little old house they were just finishing fixing up that would be just perfect! I asked her for the address and she began to answer me like the drug store preacher guy. I stopped her and asked her to write down the address instead of giving me directions using historical landmarks.

I found some wonderful maple bars and splurged on a raised donut with chocolate frosting and German chocolate frosting stuffed in the center. That was, for sure, the most sugar I'd had for a week. So to combat the sugar splurge, I spent a few minutes in the fruit and vegetable section. I went to the checkout aisle, where I was greeted by another happy lady who must also work for the local news. I was starting to become alarmed about giving out so much personal information when I began to listen to the other shoppers at the checkout.

They were rattling off cell numbers and addresses right along with the weather and the latest baseball scores.

After I paid for my purchases the bag boy offered to carry my groceries to my car. I told him not to worry about it, that I could take the stuff out myself. He insisted because, he said, "You parked way out there. I saw that your car was from out of state, so you don't want to haul all this out there yourself. Besides, you might drop something or smash your donuts like Betty Lou did last week."

That's when I knew that I had made the right decision to try to stay in this town. If I was ever going to get along here, I would need to work where I can meet lots of people, learn their names, and probably learn more than I really wanted to know. Before I looked up the address of that supposedly "darling" rental, I made another stop at the drug store to apply for a job. As I entered the store I was met with a mixture of recognition, friendliness, and concern.

The druggist, who I soon learned was also the owner, was concerned that I had experienced some bad luck, or had lost something on my first visit. The lady at the grill was certain that I was not there to complain about the hamburger. She had made it herself and the same way she had been making them for *years!* And, she had seen me devour it earlier. The other employees at the drugstore treated me like I had just returned from vacation! I spoke privately with the pharmacist and applied for a job. He was incredulous that I would want a job in his store. I explained to him that I had decided to start over with my life, and this is where I wanted to begin. I had figured that the quickest way to learn about the people in this town was to work in either this drug store or the grocery store. He laughed, agreed with me and promised to get back to me.

The next year was so fun! I felt like I had returned to school. I was learning a new language, studying the current events and history of this area and participating in service projects, scarecrow contests, parades, and learning how to drive my car in twelve or more inches of snow! I was also being taught by my coworkers and neighbors about a new form of social existence. I came to the conclusion that my first exposure to this social dynamic was the grocery bagger at the grocery store. I thought my experience with him was a pleasant, one time encounter. I had no idea at the time that his attention to my situation was the norm in this town. I caught neighbours clearing snow out of my driveway with their little John Deere tractors! People at work would bring homemade treats to share with the crew. This was not the norm where I came from, that's for sure.

As the first year wore on, I became more inquisitive about the areas surrounding this little town. To be correct, this was a little town compared to Los Angeles, but the population was approximately over thirty thousand at the time. The small communities surrounding Spanish Fork wasted no time informing me, sometimes at great length and sometimes strongly, that they were their own entities, with their very own histories. Oh my! The stories they could tell. They told of Indian troubles, fire, famine, farming and families. One lesson I learned was how to tell what time of year it was just by driving down the main road into the countryside with my windows open! I quickly learned when it was time to fertilize the fields, when the chickens were ready, when the third crop of hay was up and who had an irrigation turn. But my favourite drive was when I could just barely see the lines of green crops breaking into the light and stretching for the sun.

At the end of that first year, as a fledging newcomer, I made another important decision. That "darling" refurbished little house had provided shelter from the storms and safety from unknown terrors at night. Working two jobs in fun-filled, busy stores had helped me get settled into this new culture. The low rent and two paychecks made it possible for me to live comfortably without depleting the emergency savings account I had when I left California. So, I approached one of the attorneys in town and offered my complete resume this time. At our first meeting, the attorney was mystified when he read my credentials. As he was reading, his heavy eyebrows raised and he looked up at me. I was wondering why he was so surprised.

"With this much education and experience, why have you been working in the grocery store and the drug store?" he asked. I answered, "I needed to know the people in the area first, before I would want to help them. I found that this community is filled with selfless, concerned families who are unafraid to take a stand if necessary." I got the job!

However, my education about the people, customs, languages, and genealogy continued. I was never disappointed when I would hear a story about a farmer and a rancher working together. One would cultivate the land, plant the hay, cut it and bale it in order to sell some of it at a discount to the rancher for feed for his cattle. Then the rancher would auction off the beef but hold out a prime steer for the farmer. Sometimes when the weather or the world would get in the way, the rancher would step in and take the farmer's water turn for him, or the farmer would help haul the beef to the auction. It was all in a day's work.

There were many projects that were completed this way. For example, salesman Bob, (we'll call him) wants to upgrade his sprinkler system but doesn't know how. So, he talks it over with his friend (Larry, is his pretend name). Larry is a contractor and wants to finish his basement. Larry and Bob discuss this. This means they actually talk to each other, in real life, maybe while sitting in the stands while their kids play ball. Larry knows all the ins and outs of water pressure, timers, fittings etc. He agrees to measure Bob's yard, make a list of all the supplies needed and where Bob should go to obtain all the lines and fittings. Bob will measure all the floor space in the basement, make recommendations on floor coverings and make the proper connections so Larry will be able to get a bargain price. He will also advise on the newest styles and colors. When the time comes to actually do the work on these projects, the wives and kids come over with lunch and treats for everyone. It's a win-win! It's called "shared strength."

I also loved to listen to the people talk. Women don't talk like men. For example, when the men get together and are discussing the merits of one guy's outfit, they are not discussing the proper shoes to wear with the "outfit." When the girls get together and see their friends' "outfit" they want to know how much it cost, where they got it and if it would go with her shoes. If the girls are discussing someone's new car, they are interested in how many children it will hold and what color it is.

One night, as I was taking the long way home from work, I noticed that almost all the lights were on at the big "Sports Complex," which is a euphemism for massive sports fields. So, I drove slowly around the parking lots looking for a parking space. I wondered if I needed to purchase a seasonal parking pass from the city in order to acquire a free spot. Luckily, some woman ran to her car and spun out of the lot like she had left something cooking on the stove. I suspected it must be some kind of an emergency because she was driving and yelling at her dashboard as she careened out of the lot. Without a shred of guilt, I took the empty parking spot. I aimlessly wandered into the complex.

To my surprise, the stands were full of families. There were men both young and old, grandparents of all shapes and sizes, and even more kids. Apparently I had wandered into a women's league softball tournament. I had a flashback to "League of our Own." And, these women, aged twenty to forty-ish, were not kidding around either. I saw one pitcher with a wind-up that would make Kit shudder, and the batter? Well, she wasn't a bit intimidated. This was serious softball, folks. It was difficult to tell which team the spectators were cheering for because they all sat together and talked and laughed all during the game. Sometimes, some guy on the bleachers would stand and call the referee by his first name and express concern for his eyesight. Then the women on his right would pull the guy back down and pat his leg to settle him down. All four fields had games going at the same time.

I overheard someone ask if anyone knew where her daughter was playing. She received several answers and directions to the proper field. Apparently everyone knew who her daughter was. It was dark but the children's playground was awash with bright lights highlighting little children supervised by what appeared to be siblings because they weren't really supervising at all. I just stood in the center of all four game fields and tried to get an estimate of just how many games were played each year, factoring in t-ball, coach pitch, boy and girl little league teams each, and going all the way up to men and women's adult teams. It was mind boggling! I was in a stupor as I turned around and began to head back to my car in the huge parking lot.

I was thinking about how grateful I was for a remote car key that would make my car honk for me when someone stopped me. "Yer not leavin' yet? It's just getting exciting. Go grab a burger and meet me on field four, I know they'll win this year, because if they don't, my husband says either we all move or the kids will have to change schools." I stammered, "Are the burgers here as good as Stone Drug?" "Close." She said, over her shoulder as she returned to the game.

MEMORY LANE BY
Clark Caras; February 24, 2015

So incredible how the heart and mind can work together to create the ultimate time machine. They did that exact thing for me today.

Met and had lunch today in Spanish Fork with a childhood friend, Steve Cornaby, who I think together we decided it had been more than almost three and one half decades since we had seen or talked to one another. Yet, in the blink of an eye we were both young again as were our parents, siblings and friends who we spent four hours talking about.

Those long gone to each of us were back again. And those who might soon continue and pass were young and vibrant to each of us as we shared lunch, laughter and serious friendship.

His mother was once again my den mother and we were shucking peas along the ditch bank in the cool shade of the apple trees at the end of what to our family will always be Cornaby Lane.

A lane never really walked by me or our sisters because the hayfield was all that separated us and that pretend jungle or lava field was all that separated us from a safe place and safe and wonderful friends and an almost family.

Going down memory lane must be something like a snake shedding the old and starting anew, or the elk who gains new velvet and begins to feel fresh blood push through veins not even beginning the twisted climb skyward.

All I knew as we said goodbye with the promise to talk again sooner than later, was some sort of new DNA coursing through my veins. And a look when I saw my reflection in the mirror that hadn't been there in years. And it was so worth it, even if it had vanished by night's call to sleep. Because I knew the journey of renewed and reacquainted friendship had only just today begun.

CHAPTER 7:
LANDMARK HOMES

BY PAUL BECKSTROM

1. JOHN BABCOCK HOME—191 WEST 200 NORTH
John Babcock's home was built in 1871. John Babcock was born in 1842 in Nauvoo, Illinois, to Adolphus Henry Babcock and Jerusha as their eighth child. In 1851 Adolphus Henry Babcock (born in 1800 in Middlefield, Hampshire Massachusetts) came to Spanish Fork with his wife Jerusha Jane Rowley Babcock. Albern Babcock (born in 1840 in Nauvoo, Illinois and the oldest son of Adolphus) went to help rescue the stranded handcart companies. George Babcock (born in 1831 and the fourth child of Adolphus) settled in the new town of Palmyra along the river bottoms in 1852. At one time there was a Babcock Grove where people picnicked. The John Babcock home was the first brick home in Spanish Fork and later made into an apartment where Reed Grotegut and Rowe Harrison lived. Years later Paul and Sharon O'Brien bought and remodeled it.

2. PATTERSON HOME—110 WEST 300 NORTH

The Patterson home was built in 1940. Mr. Patterson was the U&I Sugar superintendent. Next, Wendell J. O'Bryant, also a U&I Sugar superintendent and a Palmyra Stake President, lived in this house. Paul Lambert (born in 1917 in Auckland, New Zealand) and wife Ila Thomas (born in 1922 in Spanish Fork) were the next owners. He worked at Commerical Bank. Lester Ludlow, M.D., lived here, he is the great grandson of Archibald Gardner. Now it is owned by and Dr. Brent Mrs. Kathleen Hansen. Dr. Hansen was a Mayor of Spanish Fork and dentist.

3. JOSEPH CHAPPLE HOME—58 WEST 300 NORTH

Joseph Chapple was born in 1831 in Wales, and came to Spanish Fork in the late 1850s with his wife Mary Williams Chapple and baby daughter, Margaret. The three of them came to Utah in the Bunker Handcart Company 1856. He belonged to the first Spanish Fork Choir (mostly Welsh) in 1875. This choir was invited to sing at the dedication of the Salt Lake Tabernacle. He and Mary had four children and their last child, also named Joseph, was born in 1868. The son Joseph was a volunteer firemen from the first organized Spanish Fork fire department in 1908.

4. GEORGE CHAMBERS HOME—35 WEST 300 NORTH

George Chamber's home has cement pillars that were made at the Robertson Stebbins cement plant. George was born in England in 1839. While coming with his family to Utah his father died while in Nebraska in 1853. In 1862 he married Rachel David in the Endowment House in Salt Lake City. Rachel was born in Wales coming with her family who settled in Spanish Fork in the early 1860s. George and Rachel had twelve children, raising nine to adulthood. In 1874 George Chambers and his sons established the third brick kiln in Spanish Fork. The City Hall on the Public Square was built from their bricks. In 1911 Dr. E.G. Hughes and Dr. Joseph Hughes of Spanish Fork equipped the second floor as a hospital. Later it became the Williams Apartments and the Peterson Apartments. It is currently owned by the Morris Family of Confetti Antiques.

5. DR. JOSEPH HUGHES HOME—91 EAST 300 NORTH

Dr. Joseph Hughes was born in Spanish Fork in 1876 to Morgan and Hannah David Hughes both coming from Wales separately and then marrying in Spanish Fork in 1853. The son, Joseph, married Delila Rebecca Gardner who was a daughter of Neil Gardner and granddaughter of Archibald Gardner. They bore and raised eight children in this home. The hospital was moved and attached to the original Hughes family home. Dr. Hughes was a doctor for many years and delivered many babies. He was on the first library board, and was the first Kiwanis President.

6.   MORGAN HUGHES HOME—190 NORTH 200 WEST

Morgan Hughes' home was built in 1856 from adobe and was originally two rooms; five rooms were later added. This is probably the oldest of the adobe homes left in Spanish Fork. Morgan Hughes was born in 1824 in Wales and died in Spanish Fork in 1890. He came to Palmyra in 1851 and moved to the new sight of Spanish Fork in 1856. Shortly after, he built the two rooms of adobe of this house. The walls were 18 inches thick, the doors were so small they had to be enlarged later. The house was built in the traditional saltbox style. A salt-box home has two stories on the front and one on the back. Dr. Preston and Maurine Hughes lived here for several years.

7.   BEN R. STAHMAN HOME—190 NORTH 200 WEST

Ben R. Stahman came to Utah from Minnesota in 1907. He was a photographer and ran a studio for twenty-four years. His wife, Lydia Soeffner, was the Spanish Fork candidate for state Mother of the Year. Their son Dr. Ben R. Stahman collected the first specimen of the weed Halogeton, the first recorded discovery of the plant in the United States. It was a serious threat to animals on range lands.

8.   JOHN E. BOOTH HOME—14 SOUTH 100 WEST

John E. Booth was mayor of Spanish Fork for four terms until 1941. He was born in Spanish Fork in 1895 to

Charles and Annie Booth who had come from England and raised eight children here. His wife, Beatrice Jane McKell, was also born in Spanish Fork. He was on the draft board during WWII and was the State Commander of the American Legion in 1924. He was a pharmacist with Alma Jensen who started the first World Drug on corner of 200 North Main. John bought World Drug in 1917. He also bought the Orem.

9. WALTER J. WILDE HOME—102 SOUTH 100 WEST

Walter James Wilde married Jeannette Lewis who was the fourth of eight children born to William and Sarah Ann Lewis of Spanish Fork. After their marriage and after having two children, they came to settle in Spanish Fork. They had two more children and raised them all in this house having bought this home after opening the Excel Furniture Company on the corner of Main and 2nd North which was very successful. Walter J. Wilde in 1935 invented a turn signal to be mounted on the back of a car known as the Auto-cop Electric Signal. It waved two little flags to attract a person's attention and also displayed an arrow to point the direction the car was turning and was operated from the dash. Walter had one installed on his own car. It became mandatory on large trucks and buses where arm signals could not be seen.

10. JIM CREER HOME—138 SOUTH 100 WEST

James Creer and his wife Margaret Snell Creer were both born in Spanish Fork, Jim in 1862 and Margaret in 1860. Jim's parents had nine children and Margaret's parents had fifteen children, all raised in Spanish Fork. Jim and Margaret had three children raised in this home. Jim Creer owned a harness store which was sold in 1889. He built a two-story building with Lars Nielsen which was the R.L. Jex store and it is still standing. A.E. McGlone who was superintendent of the Del Monte Cannery in Spanish Fork bought this home. It was later bought by Ray and Joyce McGlone Nielsen.

11. ROGER CREER HOME—166 SOUTH 100 WEST

Roger Creer is the son of William and Sarah Jane Creer who were born in England and raised their nine children in Spanish Fork. Roger married Delilah Bradford who was born in 1879 to Pleasant and Jane Bradford. Roger and Delilah had nine children, three died in infancy, six were raised in this home. The Roger Creer home was built in 1901. Roger Creer bought the Spanish Fork Cannery at a sheriff's sale with A.R. Creer and Charles Creer. Roger was Post Master until his death in 1945. The next owner was Fred Ludlow, a sheep man, his wife being a granddaughter of Archibald Gardner. Fred's sons, Enoch and Lester, were doctors.

12. JOHN PRESTON CREER HOME—186 SOUTH 100 WEST

John Preston Creer was a son of William and Sarah Jane Creer being born in Spanish Fork in 1904. J.P. married Mary Elizabeth Brockbank who was born in Spanish Fork in 1879 to Samuel and Mary Jane Brockbank. They raised six children in this home. John Preston taught classes in the first high school held in the garret of the Central School in 1904. J.P. Creer was the vice president of the Koyle Mining Company; in 1914 he was the superintendent of schools retiring in 1919. He was the only Republican elected in Utah County. An attorney for twenty years, Ralph Henry Andrus, later bought the home. Ralph is a grandson of Archibald Gardner.

13. CREER HOME—196 SOUTH 100 WEST

William Creer was born in Lancashire, England to Edwardand Ann Creer; he being their oldest child. By the time 201 Edward and Ann came to Spanish Fork in 1857 they had eleven children and their twelfth, Ann, was born in 1857 after their arrival. A year later, in 1858, William married Sarah Jane Miller, an English girl. They had nine children, eight living to adulthood. Their eighth child J. Preston Creer was born in this house.

14. BENJAMIN ARGYLE HOME—81 WEST 100 SOUTH

Benjamin Argyle was born in England in 1843 and married Jane Robertson in 1881. Jane was the daughter of William and Eliza Robertson who settled in Spanish Fork in 1853. They had eleven children who were raised in this home. Benjamin Argyle was appointed city marshal in 1890. In 1892 he became the vice president of the first bank in Spanish Fork named the Bank of Spanish Fork. In 1895 he opened a drug store with Jacob Robertson on Main between First and Second North where they had the first telephone in Spanish Fork. In 1896 his wife was a leader for the fight for prohibition in this area. Benjamin Argyle was elected mayor in 1899. Isaac Taylor lived here in the 1940s.

15. HENRY A. GARDNER/ED FIRMAGE—90 WEST 100 SOUTH

Henry Gardner was born to Henry Gardner and Elizabeth Martel Gardner in 1887 in Spanish Fork. He married Grace Brockbank who was also born in Spanish Fork in 1889. Henry, a grandson of Archibald Gardner, was a cashier of the newly opened First National Bank in 1928, resigning at the merger of the First National Bank and Commercial Bank in 1930 when the Bank of Spanish Fork was organized and Henry became the cashier. He became the President of the newly created Palmyra Stake in 1924. He died in 1948.

16. DR. JOSEPH HUGHES HOME—74 WEST 100 SOUTH

Dr. Joseph Hughes was born in Spanish Fork in 1876 to Morgan and Hannah Hughes. Morgan and Hannah had come to Spanish Fork in its beginnings in 1853.

The family was known by everyone. He married Delilah Gardner who also came from a known family, her grandfather being Archibald Gardner who settled in 1854 in Spanish Fork. Joseph was a doctor for many years and delivered many babies. He was on the Stake High Council the first library board, and the first Kiwanis President. Dr. Enoch Ludlow purchased the home and raised his family there. Enoch was mayor from 1982-1986. He began his medical practice in 1956. He also is a great-grandson of Archibald Gardner.

17. OWEN A. HODGE HOME—53 WEST 100 SOUTH

David Hodge was born in 1877 in Lehi, Utah. He worked for U&I Sugar Company. He and his wife had six children, one dying young, in Sugar City, Idaho. They came to Spanish Fork for his job but he died in 1935. His wife Rowena Tanner Hodge lived in this home with her two youngest children. Also this home was owned by Max Thomas, a banker. Currently it is owned by Mike Allen who owns All-n-Wood furniture restoration business.

18. DR. WALDO HAGAN HOME—41 WEST 100 SOUTH

Dr. Hagan came from Fairview, Utah, in 1909 with his wife, Clementeen, and baby. They had four more children born and raised in this home. Dr. Hagan had his office above Booth World Drug Store which was also the bus stop for some of the bus lines in Spanish Fork. He gave 44 years to his medical practice and by horse made his house calls. Payment for these calls was often given in produce such as eggs, fish, and garden vegetables. He was the first president of the Rotary Club in Spanish Fork in 1921.

19. OWEN L. BARNETT/DR. WELLS BROCKBANK HOME—70

West 100 South This home was built by the Nebo School District in 1937 for $6,000 in federal funds with Owen L Barnett as Superintendent. It was then sold to Dr. Wells E. Brockbank, a prominent doctor who practiced medicine for many years. Dr. Brockbank was born in Spanish Fork in 1891 to Samuel and Mary Jane Thomas Brockbank. The Brockbank family settled in Spanish Fork in 1853 coming from England. He married Kathryn Evans who was also born in Spanish Fork, her family coming from Wales in 1884. Dr. Brockbank was also the Mayor of Spanish Fork from 1962-1966.

20. DAVID JONES HOME—143 SOUTH MAIN STREET

The David Jones home was built in 1912. David was born to Llewellyn and Alice Creer Jones in 1887 in Spanish Fork. The Jones family had come to Spanish Fork in 1868 from Wales. Llewellyn and Alice had sixteen children and David was their twelfth child. David married Mary Nielsen, the daughter of Peter and Kirsten Nielsen who had settled in Spanish Fork in 1867 from Denmark. David Jones was a city councilman from 1933-1936 and was on the Spanish Fork Police

Force. He was a state senator. Now it is owned by J. Preston Hughes and wife Elaine Jones.

21. Isaac Brockbank Home—174 South Main Street

The Isaac Brockbank home was built in 1913. Isaac was the eighth child of Joshua A. Brockbank who came from England with his father's family and eleven children and settled in Palmyra in the early 1850s. Isaac was born in Spanish Fork in 1882. Isaac was an attorney and moved to Provo after his first wife died. Next owning the home was Pratt Thomas, a banker at Commercial Bank. He started in 1914 with Bess Gardner Hales, just the two of them. He along with Joe Hanson was involved in construction of two grain elevators between First North and Center Street (west of Main Street). The Carlson brothers later bought these grain elevators. Roy Hanson, banker-farmer, was the third owner.

22. Oran A. Lewis Home—187 South Main Street

This home was built by Sigurdur Thor Leifson, who was a ship's carpenter in Iceland and came to the Utah territory in 1884 from Iceland. The finish work was done by Erick Hanson, who also came from Iceland. Oran A. Lewis was a businessman in Spanish Fork. Oran and his wife Laura Larsen Lewis had nine children in Spanish Fork, two dying in infancy. Archie and Fern Lewis Brockbank raised their family in this home. They rented "tourist rooms" from this home. Paul had his first piano lesson from Fern Brockbank here. It was then sold to the Walker family for a mortuary.

23. DAVID P. FIRMAGE HOME—230 SOUTH MAIN STREET

David Firmage came to Spanish Fork in 1927 to manage the J.C. Penney store when his brother Ed moved to Provo. He and his wife Florence Jones Firmage raised three children in this home. Ivan and Lenore Carlson bought the home, he was in the turkey industry. Currently it is owned by the Bushman Family.

24. DR. R.C. SWALBERG HOME—255 SOUTH MAIN

Dr. Ralph C. Swalberg and his wife Sena Maranda Christiansen Swalberg came to Spanish Fork with their five children by way of Gunnison, Utah. Dr. R.C. was a veterinarian by profession. He built this home in 1930. He served as mayor of Spanish Fork from 1938 to 1940, after serving on the city council from 1934 to 1936. He was the manager of the Utah State Junior Livestock Show and became director of the Utah State Fair Board. Paul Johnston is the current owner.

25. HUBBARD TUTTLE, SR. HOME—296 SOUTH MAIN STREET

Hubbard Tuttle, Sr. obtained property from A.K. Thurber in 1878 and built a home and hotel. Hubbard was city marshal in 1890. He built a dance hall between 3rd and 4th North on the west side of Main Street. He was a partner in a cannery with Reese James on 4th South and

Main. He died in 1911.Haswell Tuttle, his son, had the property for a time then sold it to Thomas D. Measom in 1917. Jim Measom bought it in 1929 and put a gas station and small store in front of the property on 3rd South and Main. Bud Bates from Springville rented and built the Arctic Circle in front, he sold this business to Glade Schwartz in 1952 which is now Glade's Drive-In. Glade was the Chief of Police. Brent Johnston took over as manager and in 1995 Brent Johnston took over.

26. NATHANIEL LUDLOW HOME/GEORGES HOSPITAL—11 EAST 300 SOUTH (This home has been demolished. The home became Swans Market.)

Nathaniel Ludlow built this home in 1920. Enoch and Lavina Ludlow were from Yorkshire, England, and came with their three children to live in Benjamin in 1878. Their first child born in America was Nathaniel Ludlow. They later had five more children making nine in total. Nathaniel was mayor from 1924 to 1925. Dr. S.W. Georges bought the house and made it into a hospital. He came to Spanish Fork in 1932 and was born in Persia. The Stolworthys built a motel out of the hospital.

27. BENJAMIN ISAAC HOME—318 SOUTH 100 EAST

Issac was born in Wales in 1825 and came to Spanish Fork in the late 1850s with their five daughters. He and Phoebe moved into their home in 1869. In all, Benjamin and Phoebe had ten children. He was a brick layer and plasterer. He did the brick and plaster work on the Central School now the city offices. He had the first telegraph office in Spanish Fork in a room in this house.

28. Niel L. Gardner Home—103 East 400 South

Niel Gardner was the grandson of Archibald Gardner through his son Neil Gardner. Neil Livingston Gardner married Annie Elizabeth Thomas Davis, a girl who had come from Merthy Tydfil, Wales, with her family. Neil and Annie had seven children and raised them in this home. The home was built on the foundation of an old store run by Serena Evanson Gardner, one of Archibald's wives. It has the distinction of being one of the first homes in Spanish Fork to have electricity and indoor plumbing. Archibald Gardner built sawmills from Star Valley, Wyoming, to St. George, Utah. He had several wives. He built the Gem Roller Mill in Spanish Fork. He has a large posterity here in Spanish Fork.

29. Brigham Gardner Home—135 East 400 South

Brigham Gardner was a grandson of Archibald Gardner and the fifth of thirteen children of Neil and Ingeborg Evensen Gardner. Brigham married Margaret Barclay and all his nine children were born and raised in this home. His home was always attractive and well-kept. He kept bees and grew sugar cane for his own molasses and had a well for the drinking water. They were strong members of the Mormon church living in the First Ward in Spanish Fork. His fifth child, Mark Barclay Gardner, inherited the home and his son Bob owns it at this time.

30. NIEL GARDNER HOME—399 SOUTH 200 EAST

Niel Gardner is the sixth of fourteen children of Archibald and Margaret Livingston Gardner. He was born in Ontario, Canada in 1841. He had thirteen children of his own with Ingeborg Evensen all being born in Spanish Fork from 1864 to 1888. He was the director of the Spanish Fork Co-op and ardent supporter of prohibition. He was instrumental in getting water from the White River. Water was then sold to the East Bench Irrigation Company. Archibald lived in the home at times. Henry Gardner was born here. Tommy Santon lived in the home. He owned one of the first autos in Spanish Fork which he had won in the late 1930s. Chloe Gardner Moulton who was a great-granddaughter of Archibald added the front rooms.

31. JOHN SNELL HOME—111 EAST 300 SOUTH

The John Snell home was built by Sigurdur Thor Leifson from Iceland and the father of J. Victor Leifson who also built homes in Spanish Fork. Russell Johnson, who worked for Etta Beck, built the store and gas pump out front of the home. At one time Willis Hill owned the home and was the elementary principal while running the store. A family by the name of Patterson owned the home for a time. The next owner was Albert Price and called it "The Pump" and sold fuel as well as having the small convenience store. Johnny Harrison and his wife Alice then purchased it and have restored both the store and home. It is called "Johnny's" and is a Spanish Fork Icon.

32. DR. WELLS BROCKBANK HOME—89 EAST 300 SOUTH

Wells Thomas Brockbank was born in Spanish Fork in 1891 to Samuel and Mary Jane Brockbank, both his parents having also been born in Spanish Fork in 1853 and 1856. Wells married Kathryn Evans, her parents coming from Wales. Wells and Kathryn raised their five children in this home. Dr. Wells Brockbank set up a dental practice in 1922. He was a bishop and counselor in the first Palmyra Stake presidency. He was elected to the Utah State Board of Education in 1949. His son, Paul Brockbank, was also a dentist in Spanish Fork and was the next owner. Paul's wife Mary still lives in the home.

33. HUBBARD TUTTLE, JR. HOME—90 EAST 200 SOUTH

Hubbard Tuttle, Jr. was an educator. Hubbard and his wife, Harriet Simmons, came to Spanish Fork shortly after getting married in 1873. They had eleven children, losing one in infancy, but raising ten in this lovely home. He and his wife were killed in an automobile accident at the point of the mountain.

34. SILAS SNELL HOME—133 SOUTH 100 EAST

Silas Snell was a plumber by trade. Silas was born in Spanish Fork in 1879 to Rufus and Ellen Snell. He was the sixth of ten children all born and raised in Spanish Fork. Silas married Alice Robertson who was also born in 1879 in Spanish Fork to a large family. Silas and Alice had ten children and raised them in this home. He played the character of Chief Blackhawk for many years. Both the Snell and Robertson families settled Spanish Fork in the 1850s and 60s.

35. JOSEPH WILKINS HOME—111 SOUTH 100 EAST

The Joseph Wilkins home was built in 1891. Joseph was born in Spanish Fork in 1860. His mother and father, George and Catherine Wilkins, came to Spanish Fork in 1855. Joseph married Armin Tilson in 1883 and they had eight children whom they raised in this home. In 1896 the Spanish Fork Coop opened business in Eureka and Joseph was the manager. In 1928 he was the night watchman at the Co-op when he was found lying dead on a settee in the shoe department. He had been shot and the crime was never solved.

36. CHARLES C. CREER HOME—103 EAST 100 SOUTH

William Creer and Sarah Jane Miller were married in 1858 in Spanish Fork and had nine children, one dying at a young age. All were born and raised in Spanish Fork. Charles was the third son of their seven sons. In 1917 with his brothers, A.R. Creer and R.W. Creer,

Charles bought the Spanish Fork Cannery at a sheriff 's sale and began operations in August of that year. The next owner of the Creer home was Harold Creer, who farmed and became postmaster in 1945. At the death of his uncle, Roger, Harold became a rural mail carrier in 1952.

37. DAVID E. ROBERTSON HOME—140 EAST 100 SOUTH

David E. Robertson was born in Spanish Fork in 1869 and married Rhoda Emily Snell in 1892. They had ten children, raising nine in this home one dying as an infant. The David E. Robertson home was built in 1898 from sandstone from Spanish Fork Canyon and cement blocks manufactured in a plant on 4th East and 1st North that he and Gil Stebbins owned. David was a lather, plasterer and cement worker by trade. He was the second assistant fire chief on the first fire department established in Spanish Fork.

38. A.B. ROCKHILL HOME—190 EAST 100 SOUTH

Mr. Rockhill built his home. A.B. Rockhill and his wife Martha Thomas Rockhill were both from large Spanish Fork families. Both of their families came early, the Rockhills in 1852 and the Thomases in 1862. Mr. Rockhill built several homes in Spanish Fork. Zebedee Coltrin bought the home over 100 years ago. Zebedee Coltrin was a body guard to Joseph Smith in Nauvoo and a member of Zion's Camp. Zeb lived in Palmyra in 1852 and had property inside the old Spanish Fork fort (or St. Luke), built in Spanish Fork on about 2nd South and Main. Zeb was an alderman in 1859 and was on the city council in 1861. He died July 21, 1887. The next owner was Rebecca Piper who was his granddaughter. Her grandson, David Bradford, is the current owner.

39. HENRY GARDNER HOME—584 EAST 100 SOUTH

The Henry Gardner home was built in 1880. Henry was a son of Archibald and Serena Gardner and was born in 1858 in their home on 400 South and 200 East. Henry was a city marshal, a city council member, mayor, in the state House of Representatives, and a state senator for twelve years. Henry was the first bishop of the First Ward in 1891 when four wards were created. Henry was a counsellor in the Nebo Stake presidency. He also helped start the Commercial Bank. Henry's daughter Lenore and husband Ray Gull lived in the home and then their son Gene Gardner and Blanche. Now Henry's great-grandson owns it.

40. MORRIS MARTELL HOME—587 EAST 100 SOUTH

Morris Jenkins Martell was born in Spanish Fork in 1861. His wife, Mary Almira Riley was born in Spanish Fork in 1864 and they were married in Spanish Fork in 1884. Morris' parents came from Wales in the 1850s and his wife's family came from England in the 1860s. Morris built this home and furnished it before they were married and they lived in it their entire married lives. Morris and his wife had 14 children all born in this home having been delivered by midwives Mrs. Archibald and Annie Poulson.

41. ROBERT MCKELL HOME—110 SOUTH 600 EAST

Robert McKell was a blacksmith by profession. He was born in Scotland in 1824 and came to Spanish Fork in the early 1850s and married Elizabeth Boyack. They had 13 children all in Spanish Fork. In 1883 he was the director of the Merchantile Institution (Co-op). He was the second bishop of the First Ward in 1916.

42. FIFTH WARD CHURCH—710 EAST CENTER

The Fifth Ward Church was dedicated in 1939; it took ten years to build. Arthur F. McKell was the first bishop in 1929 when the First Ward was divided and Paul Beckstrom's father, Wm C. Beckstrom, was released as bishop. The design was planned to reflect the image of an open Bible.

43. HOGAN BECKSTROM HOME—14 NORTH 700 EAST

Hogan Beckstrom was born and married in Sweden. He and his wife, Fredrika Bauer, came to Spanish Fork in 1870 with six children, having two more in Spanish Fork. He was one of the first settlers of the East Bench. He owned a full city block that he purchased in 1873. He planted mulberry trees on the south of the home for a silk industry. He built the home in 1873, he was a carpenter and farmer and he worked on the Provo Tabernacle.

44. John N. Beckstrom Home—88 North 700 East

John Beckstrom was the oldest of his family he was born in 1851 in Sweden. His father and mother, Hogan and Fredrika Beckstrom, came to Spanish Fork with their seven children in 1870, having one more child in Spanish Fork. John was a farmer and carpenter. He cleared sagebrush and made his own adobe bricks to build a two-room house that he moved into on February 6, 1876 (The two rooms are the smaller portion on the left). He married one of Jens Hansen's daughters, Mary, who was born in 1858 in Spanish Fork. She was one of the first girls to be born here. John and Mary raised eleven children in this home.

45. Oran A. Lewis Drugstore—710 East 400 North

Oran Lewis had a campsite at this location with fruit trees in 1887. In 1888 he built a drugstore on East Main between 2nd and 3rd North. He moved the drugstore here in 1889; he then later moved it back to Main Street. He married Laura Larsen and they raised thirteen children in Spanish Fork. The area where this home is was known as "Little Denmark." Four of their children were born here.

46. Jens (James) Hansen Home—491 East 400 North

This home was built in 1864 as a two-story home initially. Jens arrived in Salt Lake City in October of 1854. He moved to Spanish Fork in 1858. He was a farmer and cattleman. He was a polygamist with fourteen wives. He had a school in his home. He served four missions to his native country in Denmark. It was said that he had a wife for every window and a child for every pane. At one time three of his great-grandsons were mayors of their respective cities: Brent Hansen in Spanish Fork, Gary Hansen in Payson and Mr. Wiles in Orem.

47. Margaret Thomas King Home—764 North 700 East

This was one of the first homes in Spanish Fork to have electricity which was in 1910. Daniel and Margaret Thomas King had seven children in Spanish Fork with only three living to adulthood. Margaret told about milking the cow, then taking the milk to the store early in the morning to exchange for script to be used for their groceries. She and her children gleaned wheat from the fields to trade at the mill for flour. Margaret's children honoured their mother and her hard work by building this home for her. Margaret Roach and Howard Zabriskie lived here for many years.

48. Joe Hanson Home—193 East 700 North

Joseph Hanson was born in Spanish Fork in 1874 to Henry and Anna Janson who came here in1868. Joe married Elizabeth Williams who was also born in Spanish Fork in 1876. They were the parents of seven children, one dying in infancy. Joe Hanson was one of the original organizers for the Commercial Bank. He was mayor of Spanish Fork in 1921. He became the manager of the Co-op in 1923. In 1928 he was involved in construction of grain elevators behind Main Street between Center and 1st North. He was president of the East Bench Canal Company.

49. ANDREW E. NELSON/JOSEPH NELSON HOME— 303 NORTH 300 EAST

This is the old salt-box style home. Andrew E. Nelson coming from Sweden and his wife Helga Bjarnasson raised six children in this home. Andrew Nelson was the first bishop of the 4th Ward. He was a director of the Co-op. Joseph E. Nelson (his son) was born in the home. He was a lawyer and passed the Bar Exam in 1923. He was a judge for many years and a popular funeral speaker. J. Art (Joe) son of Joseph played ball at BYU.

50. ALMA HALES HOME—380 EAST 200 NORTH

Alma Hales was the fourth child of Charles and Frances Hales. His large family came to Spanish Fork in 1859. Alma married Sushannah Hodgson in 1886; Sushannah was born in 1866 in Spanish Fork. They had eleven children. Alma was a brick mason. Alma Hales helped build the World Drug, Central School, Fifth Ward Church, and Paul Beckstrom's home. The next owner was a daughter, Ethel Hales; she lived in the home until she passed away. She was the only other person with Henry Gardner when the Bank of Spanish Fork was opened in 1930. She retired in 1966. Syd Diamond remodeled adding a family room and master bedroom on the south. It is now owned by Keir and Robyn Scobes, a former bishop of the First Ward, school teacher and soldier (served in Kuwait, Iraq, and Afghanistan during war time). He is currently on the Spanish Fork City Council.

51. James Nielsen/LeRoy Whitehead Home— 214 North 300 East

This home was built in 1913. James was a postal worker, farmer and stockman. He raised fourteen children. It is currently owned by LeRoy and Kathleen Nielsen Whitehead. Kathleen was born in the home and is a daughter of James Nielsen.

52. Jensen/Jacobson/Robertson Home—88 North 300 East

Alma and Zenobia Jensen bought the property and built the home. Both Alma and Zenobia Larsen Jensen came from Ephraim, Utah, where both of their families lived after coming from Denmark. It is of clinker brick. Alma had the first World Drug store on the east side of Main Street. John Booth worked for him. LeRoy Jacobson was superintendent of U&I Sugar Company. He had a very musical family. The next owner was Victor Robertson, who was manager of J.C. Penney and later opened a café called MarDon after his two sons Mark and Don. Don and Carolyn Robertson are the current owners. He was a dentist, stake president, bishop twice, and they raised twelve children in this home.

53.   FRANK THOMAS/WILLIAMS/BRADFORD HOME—87 NORTH 200 EAST

This home was built in 1903 by Sigurdur Thor Leifson who built many of the beautiful homes in Spanish Fork. The distinctive architecture of this turnof- the-century home is apparent. Notice the stained glass, classical trim, shingles on the tower, and contrasting brick and mortar tones. Almost no changes have been made in this home. The lot was originally deeded to George Mayer by George Snell, mayor in 1874. Claude and Ruth Thomas Williams raised two children here. Paul was a doctor and Frances was the 4-H cover girl on "Modern Miss," a fashion magazine. Glade Bradford, nephew of Claude Williams, is the current owner and has done much restoration on this beautiful home inside and out.

54.   NIELSEN/CREER HOME—91 EAST 200 NORTH

Lars Nielsen built this home in 1911. Lars was born in Denmark in 1857 but came to Spanish Fork in 1866 with his family, Peter and Kirsten Nielsen. He married Mary Johanne Beckstrom, Mary J. was born in Sweden, coming with her family to Spanish Fork in 1870. They raised a large family of ten children in this home. He was a banker, ownerof buildings on Main Street, bank president, mayor several terms, and manager of the Co-op at one time. William and Ardell Nielsen Creer raised their family here. William was a farmer and cattle man. Howard and Joyce Creer are the current owners. Howard is a son of William. They have kept the home much like the original.

55. Joshua Brockbank Home—110 North 100 East

This home was built in 1869. Joshua Brockbank was born in Liverpool, England, in 1848 and came with his parents, Isaac and Elizabeth Brockbank, to Palmyra in 1852. Joshua married Sarah Ann Jex in the Endowment House in Salt Lake City, 1865. They had thirteen children, eleven living to adulthood. He was a policeman and the pound keeper. Their daughter Eliza and her husband lived in the home for several years.

56. Cornaby/Bowen/Stephenson Home—81 East 100 North

William A. Cornaby built this home. William was born in Spanish Fork in 1876, his grandparent having come to Spanish Fork in 1858. William married Christine Sterling who was born in 1879 in Spanish Fork. They raised six children here. He was the first principal of the Thurber School. Ethel Threet Bowen and her husband, Sherman, raised their family here. She had a beauty shop in the home for years. Richard and Carolyn Bowen Stephenson now own the home.

57. A.B. Rockhill Home—88 East 100 North

This home was built in 1908. The original owner was A.B. Rockhill who was born in Spanish Fork in 1871 and married Martha Thomas who was also born in Spanish Fork in 1873. A.B. and Martha had six children, raising five in this lovely home. A.B. Rockhill was a banker at the Commercial Bank, owned a prosperous saloon, hotel, restaurant, and livery stable at one time. David and Elaine Bradford now own the home.

58. Carl Marcussen Home—87 East Center Street

This home was built in 1878-79. Carl was a school teacher and builder. He was the contractor for the Central School, and the head carpenter for the Gem Roller Mill (which burnt down). Carl traded property in Sanpete County for this lot with A.K. Thurber. It was later made into apartments. Orson Brown bought the home next; he was a Chevrolet dealer. Jack Gridley bought it from Orson Brown and the Chevrolet dealership as well. Carl and Kay Hales were also owners. Western Insurance currently occupies most of the home now, with a couple of other businesses as well.

59. William C. Beckstrom Home—390 East Center Street

This home was built in 1913. William C. Beckstrom was born in 1882 in the two-room home on 7th East and 1st North. He was the third bishop of the First Ward. He was a school teacher, rural mail carrier, farmer, stockman, and banker for a year. He also owned a small grocery store just west of his house. He was secretary of the East Bench Canal Company for forty years, charter member of the Kiwanis Club in Spanish Fork and a member of the first library board in Spanish Fork and helped in getting a library started. He was named Kiwanis Club Citizen of the Year. Paul H. Beckstrom (son) obtained the home in 1979. He and his wife Mary Ellen Chapple did major renovations to beautify the home. It is Paul Beckstrom who researched all the homes for this presentation. He wanted to expound on his father's home and background.

William and his first wife, Eliza, bought the failed Iceland store with a two-room lean-to on the back and one-fourth of the block for $900. They moved a room which had been added on to the house on 7th East and added it on to the lean-to giving them three rooms behind the store. This gave them a kitchen, living room, and a bedroom. He rigged up a bell to the front door of the store so Eliza could hear it in the living quarters in back. She tended the store while he taught school.

In 1912 they broke ground on the corner for the new home. He dug the basement himself. They had their plans and Jess Braithwaite drew up the blueprints. Jess built the forms for the basement, and Ralph Higginson put in the foundation and division walls for $100. Jess Braithwaite was the carpenter overseer. Jim Jameson and Will Gardner laid the brick for $200. Gil Stebbins did the plastering and made carpentry work in the bathroom and two bedrooms.

Erick Hanson finished the kitchen, dining room, library, hall and living room. He built the kitchen cupboards, the builtin buffet, and library bookshelves—all for $200 (interesting note: after Eliza died, William married

Nena Hansen, who was Erick's daughter. Erick didn't know the work he did would be for his own daughter at the time).

In 1912-13 a transient plumber named Harwood did the plumbing. Will Pearson, an excellent painter, did most of the painting. Will and Eliza did considerable work on the staining, which Pearson had taught them how to do it. In the spring of 1913 they moved into part of the new home, where William R Beckstrom was born.

A.K. Thurber

A.K. Thurber arrived in Spanish Fork in 1851. He was a teacher in 1852-53, and was ordained a bishop in 1863. He was called on missions. He was president of the Spanish Fork Mercantile Institution when it was reorganized in 1869. In 1870 he organized a cooperative society for the production of silkworms. He had the first child, a girl, born in the community in 1852. In 1874 he was called on a mission to the Indians. This is the last we hear of him in the Spanish Fork histories. It was probably shortly after this that he traded properties with Carl Marcussen in Sanpete County. The Thurber School, built in 1909, was named after him.

60. Koyle/Schwartz Home—210 East 100 South

As Albert Henry and Charlotte Jones Koyle got along in years they built this home in the late 1920s. They had about six years together in this home before Albert died in 1935. Charlotte then lived 21 years as a widow in this home, dying at the age of 85. They had fifteen children together. Their daughter, Sarah Ellen Koyle Schwarts, also lived and raised her family here with her husband, Eugene James Schwarts. This home has been in the Koyle and Schwartz family for many years.

61. RICHARD JEX HOME—165 SOUTH 200 EAST

R.L. Jex was born in 1887 to Richard Henry Jex in Spanish Fork, being the oldest son of nine children. His grandfather, William Jex, had come from England and settled in Spanish fork in the late 1850s having eleven children all in Spanish Fork. R.L. married Sarah Lavern Sterling and had five children raising them in this house. The Jex name is synonymous with Spanish Fork as they were all prominent citizens here. The R.L. Jex General Merchandise and Groceries Store was prominently located on Main Street and known by all the citizens of Spanish Fork. Grandfather, William Jex's lumber yard was equally known in its time

62. ANNIE JOHNSON—312 EAST 200 SOUTH

Ellizabeth Ann Sterling Johnson, always known as Annie, was born (1883) in Spanish Fork to Hyrum and Mary Sterling who raised their twelve children in Spanish Fork. She married Andrew Johnson in Spanish Fork in 1905 and they had four children. Both of their families came to Spanish Fork in the 1860s, the Sterlings from Canada and the Johnsons from Denmark.

63. HOLT HOME—613 EAST 100 SOUTH

John C. Holt was born in Spanish Fork in 1856 and his wife, Annie Jensen, was also born in Spanish Fork in 1868. John's father, William, served in the Mormon Battalion and lived just a few doors away, visiting daily to the family. William was a wonderful influence on John and his family. Annie was John's second wife and they were married in 1889 having ten children and raising nine in this home (his first wife, Martha, died in 1885). The west wing of this house still has the old lodge poles and timbers in the roof.

64. JOHNSON HOME—788 EAST CENTER STREET

In 1880 Arni and Solveg Johnson came from Vestmannaeyja, Iceland, to Spanish Fork in 1879 bringing with them two children. They had nine more children, three dying very young. Their first home was a dugout and Arni's job was helping a farmer clear his land of sagebrush. His pay was a halfbushel of grain per day. Arni finally got a job working for the railroad. He left in the spring and did not return home until after their son, William, was born in November. During this time he had saved quite a lot of money with the idea of returning to his beloved Iceland but changed his mind and bought this home. Their grandson through the oldest daughter Svensina was Byron Geslison. He taught seminary in the Nebo School District and was known and loved by many people in Spanish Fork.

65. Sigurdur Thor Leifson Home—812 East Center

Sigurdur Thor Leifson was born in Iceland in 1859. Sigurdur worked on the bridge and a building for the Denver Rio Grande Railroad and this enabled him to have enough money of $75 for the lot to build this house. It was one-fourth of the city block. He and his wife, Hjalmfridur (called Freda) Hjalmarsdottir, met in Spanish Fork and married in 1893, having six children. They spoke their native Icelandic language in the home. This helped their children to become quite fluent in Icelandic. Their oldest child, Victor, wrote a wonderful autobiography with interesting stories of his life and life of the family.

66. Kelly Jameson Home—886 East Center

Kelly Jameson was born in Iceland in 1865 and cameto America in 1884 with seven of his siblings. His wife Sigrid Runolfsdotter was born in 1869 in Iceland coming with her family in 1881. They were married in 1896 in Spanish Fork and had nine children all being raised in this home. Their children were educated in the Presbyterian School on 2nd North and 1st East.67.

67. Ole Olson Home—868 East 200 South

Ole Olson was born in Iceland in 1870 and at the age of 22 came alone to Spanish Fork where he met the girl he had fallen in love with back in Iceland, Thordjorg Magnusdotter, so they were married in 1892. She had come to America with her family a year earlier. He made $1.25 a day when he bought this lot and built their home. They raised seven children in this home. Thordjorg was affectionately called Topa. Ole worked for the Co-op Store in Spanish Fork beginning in 1919 and retiring in 1940 at the age of seventy. He also served as a councilman for the city.

68.　Sigy & Hannah Johnson Home—790 East 200 South

Sigidur and his wife Hannah Arnasdottir Johnson were both born in Iceland. Hannah and her mother and three siblings, having joined the church, came from Iceland to America. Sigidur came to Spanish Fork by himself. They married and had eight children in Spanish Fork and raised them in this home.

69.　Gisle Bearnson Home—782 East 300 South

Gisle Bearnson was born in 1879 in Iceland, his parents having come to Spanish Fork shortly after his birth. He married Sarah Ann Tilley who was born in Spanish Fork in 1877. They raised their two children in this home. Gisle Bearnson donated the ground, located in the vicinity of the first settlement of Icelanders in Spanish Fork, to the placement of the Icelandic Monument.

70.　Boas Anderson Home—339 South 800 East

Boas and his wife, Catherine (Katie) Christianson were both born in Spanish Fork in 1891. Both of their parents came from Iceland to Spanish Fork in the early 1880s. They were married and had six children, raising them in this lovely home. Music was especially important in their home with Katie playing the piano and all singing together. They had a large yard with animals, many fruit trees, and a big garden. Boas died when he was 46 years old, so Katie raised her children for years by herself. The home has beautiful stained glass windows.

71. ERIKSSON HOME—690 EAST 200 SOUTH

Eyjolfur Eriksson was born in 1854 in Iceland and while working as a fisherman married Gudrun Erlendsdottir. Eyjolfur and Gudrun learned of the gospel of Jesus Christ and planned to immigrate to Utah but Gudrun was too ill when the time came so Eyjolfur came with the three children. The youngest daughter died in Iowa so only the father and two sons made it to Spanish Fork in 1882. Ejolfur built a two-room dug out home for his family in the Iceland area on 700 East. Gudrun came the next year but was in poor health and died five years later. Eyjolfur then married Jarthrudur Runolfsdottir who had been helping in their home because of Gudrun's poor health, in 1887. Jarthrudur, was born in Iceland, too. The lot around this house was large enough to have cows, sheep, and chickens as well as fruit trees with alfalfa between the trees. They raised potatoes and other vegetables and stored for winter.

72. HENRY MCKELL HOME—789 EAST 400 SOUTH

Henry James McKell was born in Spanish Fork in 1858 to Robert and Elizabeth Boyack McKell who settled in Palmyra in 1852. He was a blacksmith in Spanish Fork.

Henry married Alice Vilate Jex who was born in 1857 in Spanish Fork, her parents having come in the early 1850s. Henry and Alice lived with their eleven children in this home.

73.   JACOB HANSEN HOME—214 NORTH 700 EAST

Jacob Hansen was born in Spanish Fork in 1865 and married Margaret Ann McKell in 1889 in the Manti Temple. Margaret, known as Maud, was born in 1868 in Spanish Fork. She and Jacob had known each other all their lives and were married 1890. Jacob bought a lot up on the bench in Spanish Fork where he commenced to build them a house. Each year after they had a child until 8 children were born and all raised in this home.

74.   JOSEPH OLSON HOME—288 NORTH 700 EAST

Joseph Michael Olsen was born in Spanish Fork in 1882 to Hans and Sena Olsen who came to Spanish Fork in the 1850s from Denmark. In 1912 he married Rhoda Myrl Robertson who was born in Spanish Fork in 1894. They had eleven children. In 1918 they moved to this house where their last seven children were born. The children attended the Rees School and were in the Fourth Ward.

75.   HALES HOME—385 EAST 100 NORTH

William Parley Hales built this house. He was a brick mason and contractor and built many of the brick homes and buildings in Spanish Fork—the old Co-op and old City Hall and some of the schools. Allen "Jack"

Brimhall and Elsie Ludlow Brimhall lived in this house until he died in 1977 and the house was sold to Janet Jenson.

76. LeRoy & Lillian Koyle Home—322 East 300 South

John LeRoy Koyle was born in Spanish Fork in 1885 to John and Emily Koyle who had been in Spanish Fork since the 1850s. He married Alice Lillian Jex who was born in Spanish Fork in 1890 to Richard and Ruth Jex who also came to Spanish Fork in the 1850s. They had eight children. This home was built of adobe bricks made locally.

77. Gower Simmons Home—346 East 300 South

David Gower Simmons was born in 1885 in Spanish Fork. He married Mary Higginson in 1911 and had seven children who were raised in this home. Gower Simmons built this home in 1916. It still has the original lot and is now owned by Larry and Anna Murdock.

78. Lewis/Shepherd Home—39 South 400 East

Moses was born in 1886 in Benjamin on the west end of Spanish Fork. Lil was born in England and as a baby came to America with her parents, Alma and Emily Cox, and two older sisters. They settled in Spanish Fork. Another sister came to the Cox family in 1894. This home was built in the early 1920s. Moses and Lil Cox Shepherd raised their family of seven here. The

Shepherds bought a horse and wagon to move their furniture into this home.

79. JOE EVANS HOME—511 EAST CENTER STREET

Joseph J. Evans was born in Spanish Fork in 1863. His parents came from Wales. He
married Margaret Davis in 1885 who was also born in Spanish Fork in 1867. They had twelve children. Joe Evans built this home and raised his children here. It was said of him, "There is no night so dark nor storm so severe but what Joe Evans will come." His youngest son, B. Davis Evans and his wife Virginia lived here.

80. LLEWELYN HOME—487 EAST 100 NORTH

Bill Bonner lived here. He was a clock maker and electrician for Spanish Fork City.

81. GIL STEBBINS HOME—440 EAST 100 NORTH

Gillman Stebbins met Martha Chambers from Spanish Fork and they married in 1893, moving to Spanish Fork. They had nine children. As a vocation Gil built the first cement plant in Spanish Fork.

82. ALBERT SWENSEN HOME—490 NORTH 300 EAST

Albert Swensen was the eighth of fourteen children his parents raised in Spanish Fork, having come from Sweden in 1859. His wife Alsina Nielsen's parents were from Denmark and raised their large family in Spanish

Fork as well Albert Swensen's son Rulon and Rhea Swenson lived here as well as Cleve and Clyde Swensen.

83. GARLAND & BLANCH SWENSEN HOME—490 NORTH 200 EAST

Garland Swensen's grandparents came from Sweden and were married in Spanish Fork in 1859. In 1922 Garland married Blanche Snell whose grandparents also came to Spanish Fork in the 1850s. Children of both grandparents were raised in Spanish Fork and their parents also raised their children here. Garland and Blanche chose this lovely home to raise their children.

84. JOHN E. BOWEN/CHRISTMAS HOME—493 NORTH 200 EAST

David and Jane Foster Bowen lived in Llanelly, Carmarthen-shire, Wales, having had four children, three living, joined the Mormon Church and immigrated to America in 1855. They came to Utah under the leadership of Dan Jones as far as Iowa. They then joined the Martin Handcart Company. This home was built by David Bowen, John E.'s father. David and Jane had come to Spanish Fork in 1858 from Wales. John E. Bowen married Mary Ann Christmas in 1879. Mary Ann's parents also came from Wales. They raised three children in this home. The family still owns the home.

85. B. Jones Home—147 East 500 North

John Bevan Jones, known just "B", was a farmer, raising cattle. His father and mother were both born in Spanish Fork in the 1860s. He married Jane Huntington from Emery County and they raised five girls and one boy in this house.

86. William Henry & Katherine Phillips Bufton Home— 48 East 500

North William Henry and Katherine came from Wales settling with their family in Spanish Fork in this home in 1925. William Henry had a convenience store between 1st and 2nd South on Main Street.

87. J. Austin Cope Home—41 East 500 North

James Austin Cope married Florence Annetta Fairbanks in the Salt Lake Temple on 1941 and they settled in Spanish Fork in 1946. He was elected as Utah County assessor and served seven years as Spanish Fork postmaster. He was the bishop of Seventh Ward in Spanish Fork and Palmyra Stake president, later becoming the stake patriarch as well as a sealer in the Provo Temple. He and Florence had twelve children who were raised in this home.

88. Daff Bowen Home—650 North Main Street

Daff Bowen owned and operated a grocery store in Spanish Fork known as Bowen Market. Frank McKell worked for Daff for many years and then took over the store when Daff died. It was located between second and third north on main street on the west side.

89. Mark Bowen Home—682 North Main Street

Charles Dixon (Commercial Bank) lived here for a while. C.O. Claudin bought and made a mortuary out of it. Mark and Ruth Paxman Bowen lived there. A son of Daff Bowen lived next door.

90. Palmer/Olson Home—647 North Main Street

This home was built in 1930 by Palmer who had a grocery store in downtown Spanish Fork. Jane Olson lives in it now.

91. Peterson/Allred Home—395 North 200 East

Soren Petersen was a furniture maker and had a shop at 4th North between 1st and 2nd East. Mr. Petersen made coffins and caskets which was a very necessary service at a time when there were no undertakers and ready-made caskets were not available. He made the coffins hexagonal, wide at the top to accommodate the shoulders and tapered to the feet. Soren and his wife Margretha Rigtrup had ten children in this home, raising eight to maturity. Their last son, Heber Alvin, married Astrid Nilsson and also lived in this house. Then, Heber's daughter, LaNora married Grandin Allred and they lived in the home until their deaths in

2005. LaNora and Grandin added an addition to the house but otherwise tried to keep it as it was originally.

92. JIM & HANNAH SWENSON HOME—350 NORTH 200 EAST

James Heber Swenson was born in Spanish Fork in 1879, his parents having joined the church in Sweden in 1853 and coming to Zion. Jim married Hannah Snell who was also born in Spanish Fork in 1883. Jim and Hannah raised four children in this home. Jim had architecturally planned and built this home for his family. Their daughter Martha, who was a school teacher, married Clarence B. Eaton and raised their children here. Their son Jimmy was the local veterinarian. This home is made of clinker brick which has a rough surface.

93. PETER LARSEN HOME—190 EAST 300 NORTH

Peter and Johanne Larsen joined the church in April of 1867. They brought their five children to America and settled in Spanish Fork, having six more children living in this home.

94. NEPHI SWENSON HOME—207 EAST 300 NORTH

Nephi and Emma Swenson raised their family in this home. Nephi was born to August and Sarah Swensen who had joined the church together in Sweden in 1853 coming to America in 1866. Nephi's wife, Emma Christensen's parents joined the church in Denmark in 1858 coming to Salem to settle. Clair Swensen was raised in this home.

95. SAMUEL CORNABY HOME—163 EAST 100 NORTH

Samuel and Hannah Cornaby joined the Church of Jesus Christ of Latter-day Saints in England in 1852 and came to America in 1856 to be sealed in the Endowment House that same year. They had four children with only two still alive when they came to Spanish Fork in 1859 to settle. They raised their family in this home. The older section was made with adobe bricks hand made by the family. Three more children were born in this house. George and Alta Ludlow Larsen raised their family here as well.

96. R.L. JEX HOME—145 NORTH 100 EAST

R.L. Jex built this home and lived in it for a time. R.L. owned and operated the R.L Jex General Merchandise business on Main Street in Spanish Fork and was the founder of the Bank of Spanish Fork in 1930. His wife Sarah LaVern Sterling Jex was always his support. When his youngest daughter, Esther, married Robert Bohne, they moved in and raised their family. This home is still in the family, as it is owned by their son Allen today.

97. BENT BROWN HOUSE—144 EAST CENTER

Benton Hart Brown came from a family of seven children, he being the oldest. His mother and father moved to Spanish Fork in 1876 and raised all of their children here. He married Louise Jonsson, a daughter of Jon Jonsson. Jon Jonsson was from Vestmannaeayjar, Iceland, and one of the first Icelanders to come to

America coming in 1859. Bent and Louise raised nine children in this home. He ran a livery stable which provided bed and board for horses and buggies for hire. The livery stable was on 1st North between Main and 1st East. In 1874, dried adobes were replaced by the first bricks made in Spanish Fork made by Carl Grotegut, Sr., at the Snell farm in the river bottoms. Grotegut had learned brick making in Germany. He made the bricks for this Benton Brown home.

98. WILLIAM & MAHALIA MARTEL HOME—166 EAST CENTER

William Martel was the fourth child of ten children, born in 1839, to Thomas and Eliza Martel. Both parents were from Welch families. William married Mahalia Mary Kearns in 1896 and they raised three children in this home. He was the first rural postman in Spanish Fork. He delivered mail to Palmyra, Lake Shore, Leland, and Benjamin. Later Manuel and Jessie Roach Clayson raised their family here.

99. JONES HOME—210 EAST CENTER

In 1862, William R. Jones and his wife Mary Ann Stevens Jones came to settle in Spanish Fork after a few years of living in other Utah towns. They both were born and raised in Merthyr Tydfil, Wales. They had five children, two having died while still in Wales. Four more were born and all raised in Spanish Fork having come here in the 1850s. William R. Jones was given the original deed, which was granted by the mayor of the city, in 1873, being lot number 3 which is on the northwest corner of block number 34.

100. BANKS/CHRISTENSEN HOME—249 EAST CENTER

Jon Johnson and his wife Anna were Icelanders who came across the plains in 1859. They had ten children raising them in Spanish Fork. Their seventh child was Ellen Gudrun Johnson. She married Robert Taylor Banks who was the ninth of eleven children having settled in the 1850's in Spanish Fork. After his death in 1915 she married Mikel Hyrum Christensen in 1918 and they stayed in this home.

101. JEX/JOHN STERLING—160 SOUTH 300 EAST

R.L. Jex built this house and his wife's brother, John Sterling, lived in it. John and his wife, Jennie Gardner, raised their five children here. Jennie Gardner is a granddaughter of Archibald Gardner. John's father and mother were married in 1868 in Spanish Fork and raised their eleven children in Spanish Fork. John was the second to youngest of the family. Both John and Jennie were strongly loyal to their Spanish Fork.

102. LOUISE FROST THOMAS HOME—109 SOUTH 300 EAST

Benjamin I. Thomas and Louise Frost Thomas had three children when Ben died at 27 years old, one daughter, Marie, being born after his death. This caused Louise to raise their children alone. Both Ben and Louise were born in Spanish Fork. Ben's father was a Taylor coming in the late 1880s from Wales and Louise's father was the first custodian of the Thurber School and a mail carrier in 1864. Years later Louise met an old bachelor, Will Robertson, who said that if she would marry him he would build her a new home. They were married in 1930 and this is the home he built.

Paul Beckstrom was born to a Swedish father, William Charles Beckstrom, and an Icelandic mother, Nancy Matilda Hanson in 1927. He was born and raised in Spanish Fork, learning the value of hard work and gaining a high work ethic. He earned his Bachelors, Masters, and Doctorate Degrees in History. He was the principal of schools in Benjamin, Lake Shore, Springville, Payson and Spanish Fork. While being principal he made the effort to learn the names of every child in each of these schools. He was a people person and loved to share the local history of this area which he also loved. His memory was phenomenal for details which brought the history to life.

An old African proverb says, "Every time an old person dies it is as if a library burned to the ground." Such was certainly true on October 27th, 2011, when our beloved Paul Beckstrom passed away. Paul loved this project so much that he would arrange for the Senior Citizen's bus with Jay Rindlebaucer as the driver, to take groups like the Daughters of the Pioneers or a "ladies club" on a tour all around town while he told the stories of the families who had lived in these homes. He would accept no payment. "Oh No!" he'd say, "It's my pleasure."

Thanks also to David and Kathy Stringham who have compiled and improved on this project by taking pictures of some of the homes.

CONCLUSION

In his article for The Press [Our Town], B. Davis made an interesting observation. He titled his article: "Community Image and the Principle of giving, January 9, 1969." A mental picture is the picture that flashes through one's mind when a name of something or someone is mentioned or read. Be that picture attractive or unattractive to the recipient depends on the past or present performances of that person or thing. We now call that a mental picture an "image," and so our images are being framed in the minds of our fellow men by our words, thought and our deeds…. You know a town can have an image and it only takes a small percentage of its populaceto make that image attractive or unattractive. It all depends on the following that the percentage gets…

Do we remember when we thought of Payson as the small suburb of Spanish Fork? Payson had an accessible canyon, a race track for horse racing and a great snow sledding hill. Now, in 2015, Payson has a great swimming pool, great baseball field, and an LDS temple. They even got their Wal-Mart before Spanish Fork did! Granted, there are good amenities in both towns and in all the surrounding areas. This valley is growing in leaps and bounds.

But the most important amenity any town has is its people and the very attitude of those people. There are now and have been in years past many wonderful people who have built an image for themselves and their families that have touched many lives statewide. These are people who "work quietly in quiet places carving an image in the schools, the churches and civility."

Everyone can make his own list of the people of Spanish Fork who have shaped our lives. And each of us can strive to become like them by developing and sharing the strength of character and the willingness to serve, they taught us. This is why we are proud to call Spanish Fork "My Hometown."

As we come to the end of this study about why we stay here or why we return here in Spanish Fork, please do not reach the conclusion that we think we are better than anyone else. It's not that we have the strongest pioneer stories or the deepest grass roots. Almost everyone in town has experienced difficulties of some kind, be it allergies or afflictions, finances, or families. The difference, in my opinion, is that when someone is town sees a person with some kind of hardship, they don't skirt around that person with relief. Instead, it is more likely they will be realizing how lucky (or blessed) they are and think, "If he can handle that problem, my problem is nothing. I can get through it."

I really do love this town!

—Susan Barber

ACKNOWLEDGMENTS

Many thanks to my family, my
children and my extended
family. A special thanks to my
friends and neighbors who
had to answer many questions
about details they thought
everyone should know on places and events.

———————

Lori Bradford Barber
George Beardall
The Merrill Binks Family
Nina Child
Clark Caras
Pat Frandsen
Larry and Barbara Forsey
Steve Gardner
Wanda Gottfredson
Maxine Gordon
Mark Harrison
Lane Henderson
Douglas Houghton
Sharlene Irvine and family
J-Mart Publishing
Roy and Colleen Johns

Lynn Jones
Melba King
Cathy Larsen
Ruth Leifson
Pam G. Mendenhall
Steve Money
Nebo School District
Dave Oyler
Mr. and Mrs. Don Robertson
Janet Sidman
Spanish Fork City
Spanish Fork Police Dept.
Spanish Fork ambulance crew and Don Thomas
David and Kathy Stringham
Jack Swenson
Morgan Warner
Steve Wilson

ABOUT THE AUTHOR

Even though Susan was raised in Denver, She finished school in Marseille, France and then attended BYU.

She and her husband owned and operated an Insurance Agency in town and both served in civic organizations for years. As a hobby, Susan coaches interview skills to young men and women in preparation for employment opportunities.

This is Susan's second book. Her first book, Widows 101, was written as a source of information for the often unprepared new widow.

Printed in the United States
By Bookmasters